New Testament Survey

James L. R. Catron

EMMAUS
INTERNATIONAL

Developed as a study course by Emmaus Correspondence School, founded in 1942.

New Testament Survey
James L. R. Catron

Published by:
  Emmaus International
  PO Box 1028
  Dubuque, IA 52004-1028
  phone: (563) 585-2070
  email: info@emmausinternational.com
  website: EmmausInternational.com

Revised 2004 (AK '04), 2 Units
Reprinted 2007 (AK '04), 2 Units
Reprinted 2012 (AK '04), 2 Units
Revised 2015 (AK '15), 2 Units
Revised 2019 (AK '19), 2 Units

ISBN 978-1-59387-480-3

Code: ER10NTS

Copyright © 1996, 2004, 2015, 2019 Emmaus International

All rights in this course are reserved. No part of this publication may be reproduced or transmitted in any manner, electronic or mechanical, including photocopy, recording, or any information storage and retrieval system including the Internet without written permission from the publisher. Permission is not needed for brief quotations embodied in critical articles and reviews.

Scripture quotations are from the ESV® Bible (The Holy Bible, English Standard Version®), copyright © 2001 by Crossway, a publishing ministry of Good News Publishers. Used by permission. All rights reserved.

Printed in the United States of America

Course Overview

The Bible is a big book covering many centuries of history, cultures, and people. Despite the size and diversity of the Bible, the writers of the New Testament claim that Jesus Christ stands as the center and climax of all of Scripture (Luke 24:25-27). Each of the 27 books of the New Testament support this claim in their own way. These books are written to different audiences in unique contexts and by different authors in diverse situations, yet all of them place Jesus Christ at the heart of world history as the Savior who brings salvation and forgiveness to all who follow Him.

This course will briefly survey each book of the New Testament, giving its context, outline, major themes, and brief description of its content. The purpose is for you to gain a general understanding of how each book fits into the bigger picture of the Bible, and how all of it points to Christ.

Lessons You Will Study

Student Instructions

This Emmaus course is designed to help you *know God* through a *better understanding of the Bible* and *how it applies to your life*. However, this course can never take the place of the Bible itself. The Bible is inexhaustible, and no course could give the full meaning of its truth. If studying this course is the end goal, it will become an obstacle to your growth; if it is used to inspire and equip you for your own personal study of the Bible, then it will achieve its goal. As you study the Bible using this course, prayerfully ask God to reveal His truth to you in a powerful way.

Course Sections

This course has three parts: the *lessons*, the *exams*, and an *exam sheet*.

The Lessons

Each lesson is written to help explain truths from the Bible. Read each lesson through at least twice—once to get a general idea of its content, and then again, slowly, looking up any Bible references given. You should always have your Bible opened to the verses or passage being studied. It is important that you read the Bible passages referenced, as some questions in the exams may be based on the Bible text.

To look up a Bible verse, keep in mind passages in the Bible are listed by book, chapter, and verse. For instance, 2 Peter 1:21 refers to the second book of Peter, chapter 1, and verse 21. At the beginning of every Bible, there is a table of contents which lists the names of the books of the Bible, and tells the page number on which each book begins. For practice, look up 2 Peter in the table of contents and turn to the page number listed; then find the chapter and verse.

The Exams

At the end of each lesson, there is an exam to assess your knowledge of the course material and the Bible passages. The exams contain multiple choice and/or True/False (T/F) questions. After you have studied a lesson, complete the exam for that lesson by recording your answers on the exam sheet at the end of the course. If you have difficulty answering the questions, re-read the lesson or use the Bible as a reference.

Please note, it is best not to answer the questions based on what you *think* or have *always believed*. The questions are designed to find out if you understand the material in the course and the Bible.

What Do You Say?

In addition to the multiple choice section, each exam also contains a *What Do You Say?* question. These questions are designed for your personal reflection and to help you express your ideas and feelings as you process the lesson's content. Your responses should not be written on the attached exam sheet, but rather, directly written in the space provided at the end of each exam.

The Exam Sheet

Use the exam sheet included at the end of the course to complete the exams. When you have determined the right answer to a question on an exam, fill in the corresponding letter on the exam sheet. If you have an Emmaus Connector and he/she provides a different exam sheet, please use that one instead.

Write It Out!

The exam sheet also contains *Write It Out!* questions. These questions are designed to help you apply the course's content to your daily life.

Continued on next page

Write It Out! (continued)

The *Write It Out!* questions will address your *head* (thinking), *heart* (feeling), and *hands* (doing).

1. **Head.** The first *Write It Out!* question will be geared toward your head and asks you to respond to a critical question concerning the course in its entirety.

2. **Heart.** The next question asks how the course affects your perspective of or feelings toward God, yourself, or others.

3. **Hands.** The final question asks you what action you need to take in response to what you have learned.

Write It Out! questions will be reviewed and responded to by an Emmaus Connector, an official partner of Emmaus International who is trained to encourage and guide you with their response.

Prayer Requests or Questions?

You may include your personal questions on the exam sheet to help us get to know you and your needs better. Please let us know specific questions you may have about the Bible, God, or other spiritual matters. You may also include a personal prayer request and we will pray for you.

Submitting the Exam Sheet

When you have answered all the exam questions on the exam sheet, check them carefully. Slowly tear out the exam sheet along the perforated edge near the course spine. Please note, do not tear out the exams from the lessons; submit the *exam sheet only*.

Fill in your contact information and submit your completed exam sheet to your Emmaus Connector or the organization from which you received it (several options for submission are shown at right).

OPTION 1: Send to your Emmaus Connector

If you know your Emmaus Connector, give them your completed exam sheet or mail it to the address listed here (if blank, go to option 2).

OPTION 2: Send to Emmaus International's head office

If no address is listed above, or you do not know if you have an Emmaus Connector and are unsure of where to send your exam sheet, you can:

MAIL the exam sheet to

Emmaus International
PO Box 1028
Dubuque, IA 52004-1028

OR

EMAIL a scan or photo

of both sides of the exam sheet
to this email address:

Exams@EmmausInternational.com

Receiving Your Results

You will receive your graded exam sheet back (through the same method it was submitted, either mail or email), including your final grade and personal response from an Emmaus Connector.

After finishing this course, you will be awarded a certificate of completion, which serves as official record that you studied the contents of this course. A transcript of courses you complete will be stored by Emmaus International or your Emmaus Connector.

Introduction to New Testament Survey

As I was beginning my senior year of high school, my parents gave me a gift of a Bible. This, my mother said, would be my graduation gift. Though I had begun to attend a high school Sunday School class, I was disappointed that this gift, given months before graduation, was to be my graduation present. Why did my parents not give me something practical, like money? Though I had nothing against the Bible, and in fact had some respect for it, I did not perceive this to be the best gift I could have ever received. My parents were not believers but they gave me the Bible anyway. I tried to read it occasionally, but it was difficult and boring. Little did I realize that within a few months after receiving that Bible I would actually love it and make an effort to read the whole New Testament, starting

> **Jesus Christ is the key to understanding the Bible.**

with Matthew's Gospel. Little did I realize that I would eventually give my life to the study and communication of the Bible, the Word of God. Why the change in attitude? It was due to the fact that I trusted Jesus Christ as my personal Savior on January 3, 1952. Jesus Christ is the key to understanding the Bible (Luke 24:45). He gave me a hunger and thirst for the Word of God. I still have that hunger and thirst some 42 years later. He can do the same for you. As you read this book and the appropriate Scriptures which go along with each lesson, I trust that you will grow and mature in your faith in Christ. I trust that God our Father will not only give you an increasing hunger for the Bible, but for practical application of the Scriptures to your life.

Background to New Testament Survey

The New Testament was written over a 50-year period of time (AD 45–95). This is very brief in contrast to the Old Testament which was written over several centuries (c. 1400–400 BC). There are two portions of background which prepare a student to have a good grasp of the New Testament. The first portion is the *Old Testament* and the second is the *Intertestament Period* (between the New Testament and Old Testament). The New Testament finds its roots in the Old Testament in a primary sense, and in the Intertestament period in a secondary sense.

The Old Testament Roots of the New Testament

Without the Old Testament there would be no New Testament. One famous Biblical scholar of the fifth century AD said that "The New is in the Old concealed; The Old is in the New revealed." What did he mean by that? Among other things, he meant that the unconditional promises and prophecies of the Old Testament find their fulfillment in the New Testament. The four Gospels, for instance, demonstrate clearly that the prophecies in the Old Testament concerning the coming Messiah are fulfilled in Jesus, the Christ. The death of Jesus, for example, was prophetically described in Isaiah 53 and Psalm 22. The New Testament would be very difficult to understand in several places without a knowledge of the Old Testament. The New Testament constantly mentions people, places, institutions, ceremonies, beliefs, etc. which would be a mystery without a knowledge of the Old Testament. The Christian must not neglect the reading and study of the Old Testament. Make a reading schedule and determine to read through this first great portion of the Bible. The greater the familiarity you have with the Old Testament, the more you will be able to understand and interpret the New Testament.

The Intertestament Roots of the New Testament (400–4 BC)

With the book of Malachi the Old Testament came to a close (400 BC). Between Malachi and Matthew (400–4 BC), God did not give to the Hebrew people any further revelation. For this reason this period is sometimes called the Four Hundred Silent Years. Though silent in the sense of communicating new revelation to Israel, God was still at work during this period fulfilling His prophetic Word from parts of Daniel 8, 11, and Zechariah 9. The prophecies and their fulfillments were: (1) in the realm of the change of political powers controlling Palestine (six military governments ruled Palestine during the 400 years); (2) the persecution of the Jewish people by Gentile overlords; (3) and God's protection and preservation of Israel from physical extinction and spiritual corruption through paganism.

Many things mentioned in the New Testament, especially the Gospels and the book of Acts, find their roots in the 400 years between the Testaments. For instance, (1) the family of king Herod (Matt. 2:1, 22); (2) the Jewish Sanhedrin—Jewish Supreme Court (Luke 22:66); (3) the religious sectarian groups such as the Scribes, Pharisees and Sadducees (Matt. 2:4; 3:7) along with their religious ideas, traditions and practices (Matt. 23:1-2; 23; Acts 23:8). Then there were (4) political and militaristic groups such as the Herodians (Matt. 22:16) and the Zealots (one of Jesus' apostles had formerly been a Zealot—"Simon who was called the Zealot" (Luke 6:15). Of course (5) the Roman Empire which took over Palestine during Intertestament times (63 BC) was still in power throughout the New Testament era (Luke 2:1; 3:1; John 11:48).

The Intertestamental Period was in a sense a period of preparation for the coming of Jesus, the Christ. He came, says Paul, "when the fullness of the time had come ..." (Gal. 4:4-5). During the 400 years between the Testaments, God was at work preparing for that time when His Son, Jesus Christ, would step out of eternity into time. Note the following preparations which led to the "fullness of the time."

- *There was the preparing of the way through the Greek language.* Alexander the Great conquered the Mediterranean world and the near east (334–323 BC) in a cultural sense, as well as militarily. One very important aspect of Greek culture was the Greek language. After Alexander, the Greek language gradually became the language used everywhere. The Old Testament Scriptures were translated into Greek in Egypt between 250 and 100 BC. This translation, known as the Septuagint, was used by Jewish people scattered over the Mediterranean world who were losing their ability to speak Hebrew. In the providence of God, the Gospel was spread to Jewish people and unbelievers in the Greek language. Also, the whole New Testament was originally written in Greek.
- *There was the preparing of the way through Roman political power.* The Roman Empire brought a number of positive things which made the spread of the Gospel a reality. For one thing, the

Romans built a vast system of excellently made roads throughout the empire. Preachers of the Gospel, like Paul, took advantage of these roads to enable them to move swiftly and with ease to their destinations. Never were circumstances better or more favorable for the proclamation of the Gospel. The fact that Rome had its armies stationed throughout the empire to insure the law and order for which they were famous was a plus to the growth of Christianity.

• *There was the preparing of the way through the Hebrew religion.* During Intertestamental times Judaism developed into a highly legalistic system. This legalism continued on into New Testament times with great vigor. Legalism is man's attempt to make himself acceptable to God on the basis of self effort (law keeping). It is illustrated in the Gospels in the various encounters Jesus had with the Scribes and Pharisees (see the teaching of Jesus, for instance, in Matt. 15). Legalism was Jesus' most formidable obstacle to overcome in Judaism. However, what positive things did the Hebrew religion contribute? The answer is simple. The Hebrew religion centered around the truth of monotheism (one God), and the Law of Moses. Wherever the Jewish people went in the dispersion they took these two foundational truths. Paul took advantage of this ideal situation when he went on his missionary journeys. How? He would always go to the Jewish people first, at the synagogue, using what truth they did know as a springboard to preach the Gospel.

The Books of the New Testament

1. History
Matthew, Mark, Luke, John, Acts

2. Letters
Romans, 1 Corinthians, 2 Corinthians, Galatians, Ephesians, Philippians, Colossians, 1 Thessalonians, 2 Thessalonians, 1 Timothy, 2 Timothy, Titus, Philemon, Hebrews, James, 1 Peter, 2 Peter, 1 John, 2 John, 3 John, Jude

3. Prophecy
Revelation

There are 27 books of differing lengths, authors, content, style, emphasis, and purpose in the New Testament. They may easily be arranged into three major categories: *history, letters* (also called epistles), and *prophecy.*

1. History

The four Gospels (Matthew, Mark, Luke, John) give four different historical portraits of the Lord Jesus Christ. The English word *gospel* is derived from the Anglo-Saxon word *godespell. Gode* means "good" and *spell* means "story" or "tale." The Gospel is not just a good story, but a good story which is the good news of salvation to all mankind (Luke 2:10-11). The "good news" encompasses Christ's coming, ministry on earth, perfect life, suffering and death upon the cross for the sins of the world, His bodily resurrection from the dead, and His ascension to heaven with the promise of His return.

The writers of the four Gospels wrote by inspiration of the Holy Spirit so that we might have an accurate, purposeful, and authoritative account of Christ's life. Just as any thoughtful modern-day preacher would tailor his sermon to meet the needs of the congregation, so the writers of the four Gospels wrote their portraits of Christ's life keeping in mind the makeup and needs of those for whom they wrote. But why four Gospels? Why not just one? Or why stop at four? Why not five or even more? The fact that there are four Gospels may be accounted for by the intention of the Holy Spirit to reach four representative groups which would find their counterpart in any age. Matthew wrote to the Jewish people presenting Jesus as the promised King; Mark wrote to the Romans and portrayed Jesus as the servant of the Lord; Luke wrote to Theophilus (for the Greeks), picturing Jesus as the perfect man; and John wrote for the world with his portrait of Jesus as God. In modern times there are those to whom Mark's Gospel will have a special appeal and they will be first influenced by it. Others today may find that John's Gospel is very attractive to them and they are first affected by it, etc.

The four Gospels may be divided into two categories. The first category includes Matthew, Mark and Luke. These three Gospels are called by scholars the *synoptic* Gospels. What does that mean? Synoptic means "to see together." In other words, these Gospels take a similar approach in their presentation of the life of Jesus. John's Gospel, the second category, is very dissimilar from the first three because over 90 percent of its content is not found in the other three.

The Book of Acts is the last of the five historical books. It continues the history where the Gospels finish. Jesus ascended to heaven but His work of reaching the world continued on through the preaching of the Apostles and others. Acts reveals the new body, the church, which Jesus had predicted (Matt. 16:16-18) and which the Holy Spirit created on the day of Pentecost (Acts 2). It gives the history of the growth and development of the church from Jerusalem to Rome. It is a thrilling book recording the triumph of the Gospel throughout the Mediterranean world. During the history of the Acts period, ten of the letters (epistles) of Paul were written. James also wrote his letter during this period.

2. The Letters (Epistles)

There are 21 books of the New Testament in this category. These are divided into two sections. The first major section consists of 13 letters written by the Apostle Paul (Romans through Philemon), and the second is made up of Hebrews through Jude, which scholars have called the General Epistles.

Some of the *letters of Paul* were written to individuals to encourage them in their faith and work (1 and 2 Timothy, Titus). Some were written to particular churches to challenge their faith, pass on new truth and instruction, correct error, solve problems, and warn against evil and false teachers (1 Corinthians, Colossians, etc.). Paul's letters have a great balance of doctrinal truth and practical application to individual and corporate church life.

The designation *General Epistles* is applied to Hebrews; James; 1 and 2 Peter; 1, 2, and 3 John; and Jude. The designation is not a Biblical expression but it does appear in the title of five of the above letters in the King James Version (AD 1611). It is an old term and scholars have puzzled over its meaning without coming up with any satisfactory answer. One interesting view is that the term denotes writings which are general in nature and not addressed to any specific church. One discerns when reading these eight epistles that two of the prominent themes are (1) encouragement for Christians who are suffering persecution (Hebrews through 1 Peter); and (2) warning against false teachers and teaching (2 Peter through Jude).

By way of clarification, there has always been debate over the authorship of Hebrews. The author of Hebrews does not identify himself, but some believe it was Paul. Most, however, think it was someone else based on the author's literary style, vocabulary, method of argumentation, etc.

3. Prophecy

The book of Revelation gives a fitting conclusion to the New Testament. Though other New Testament books have some prophetic themes concerning both the church and Israel, Revelation is exclusively devoted to prophecy. John was told by Christ in Revelation 1:19 to "write therefore the things that you have seen, those that are and those that are to take place after this." Revelation majors on the judgment which God will bring upon the earth prior to the second coming of Christ, and it ends on the positive note of victory over God's enemies and the establishment of the kingdom.

The Order of the New Testament Books

The order in which we find the New Testament books in our Bible is logical rather than chronological. For instance, James was probably the first book of the New Testament to be written (AD 45), but it is 20th in the order given in the New Testament. John's Gospel was written somewhere between AD 85–95 but it is fourth in order. Galatians was written around AD 47–49, shortly after James, but it is ninth. In this study of the New Testament we shall consider each book, except Philemon and Titus, in the order in which it is placed in our Bibles. Philemon will be studied with Colossians and Titus before 2 Timothy. The first four books (Gospels) give the basic history of the founder of Christianity—Jesus Christ. This is followed by the proclamation of the person and work of Christ in the book of Acts. This in turn is followed by the interpretation of Christ's person and work in the Letters. Finally, the book of Revelation shows the consummation of all things in the second advent of Jesus Christ.

LESSON 1 EXAM

Use the exam sheet at the back of the book to complete your exam.

1. **The New Testament was written over a period of**
   A. 25 years.   C. 40 years.
   B. 30 years.   D. 50 years.

2. **The time between the two testaments is called the**
   A. silent years.
   B. prosperous years.
   C. rebellious years.
   D. dark years.

3. **God prepared the way for the coming of His Son through**
   A. the Greek language.
   B. the Roman political power.
   C. the Hebrew religion.
   D. all of the above.

4. **The books of the New Testament are arranged as**
   A. wisdom, prophecy, and history.
   B. history, letters, and prophecy.
   C. poetry, law, and wisdom.
   D. letters, prophecy, and poetry.

5. **The four Gospels give four different**
   A. periods of the Lord's life.
   B. purposes of the Lord's life.
   C. portraits of the Lord's life.
   D. powers in the Lord's life.

6. **The Holy Spirit gave us four Gospels to**
   A. make the life of Christ more exciting.
   B. fulfill the prophecy of the Old Testament.
   C. reach four representative groups of people.
   D. dramatize the fullness of Christ's life.

7. Among other things, the Book of Acts records the history of the
   A. growth and development of the church from Jerusalem to Rome.
   B. Pharisees and Sadducees.
   C. choosing of the twelve apostles.
   D. the death of the Apostle Paul.

8. **Two of the books designated as *General Epistle*s are**
   A. 1 Corinthians and Romans.
   B. Ephesians and Colossians.
   C. Hebrews and James.
   D. Galatians and Philemon.

9. **The Book of Revelation is exclusively devoted to**
   A. God's promise of world peace.
   B. the Holy Spirit.
   C. prophecy.
   D. encouragement.

10. **The order of the New Testament books is**
    A. logical.   C. chronological.
    B. topical.   D. psychological.

What Do You Say?

How would you respond to someone who says that Christ was born at the wrong time and therefore was rejected and killed?

EXAM 1

Matthew, Mark, and Luke

THE GOSPEL OF MATTHEW

Usually a book includes a brief description of the author. This biographical information may be a stimulus to read his book with more interest and enthusiasm. The New Testament does not provide us with photographs of its authors, but there is some biographical material in their books as well as some of the other books. This helps us to get to know the authors and fully appreciate what they wrote. What can we know about Matthew? When seen together, Matthew, Mark and Luke give us the following summary:

Matthew, the Man

Scripture Texts

Matthew 9:9-10	Mark 2:14-15	Luke 5:27-29
As Jesus passed on from there, He saw a man called Matthew sitting at the tax booth, and He said to him, "Follow me." And he rose and followed Him. And as Jesus reclined at table in the house, behold, many tax collectors and sinners came and were reclining with Jesus and His disciples.	And as He passed by, He saw Levi the son of Alphaeus sitting at the tax booth, and He said to Him, "Follow me." And he rose and followed Him. And as He reclined at table in his house, many tax collectors and sinners were reclining with Jesus and His disciples, for there were many who followed Him.	After this He went out and saw a tax collector named Levi, sitting at the tax booth. And He said to him, "Follow me." And leaving everything, he rose and followed Him. And Levi made him a great feast in his house, and there was a large company of tax collectors and others reclining at table with them.

His Names—Matthew, Levi

Mark and Luke call him Levi. Levi calls himself Matthew (Matt. 9:9). It is thought by Bible scholars that Levi was his family name (surname) and Matthew was his given name. Matthew means "gift of the Lord." It is not unusual for a parent to name a son "Matthew" because of what it means. It is a good name and reminds us that children are God's gift to families (Psalm 127:3-5).

His Family

Nothing is known of his family except his father's name—Alphaeus (Mark 2:14). With some of the authors of Scripture we get more family information. Evidently Matthew's family background could not contribute anything significant to the story.

His City

Matthew was from Capernaum which was located at the northern end of the sea of Galilee. Jesus settled and ministered in Capernaum (Matt. 4:13), where Matthew must have heard Him preach the Gospel more than once until he finally responded in faith and was converted.

His Occupation

Matthew was a tax collector. The Romans were in power in Palestine and often employed Jewish people to administrate the collecting of taxes. In New Testament times there were two levels of tax officials. There was the chief tax collector who contracted with the Romans to collect the taxes (Luke 19:2). Then there were those who worked under him. Matthew was on the second level. Tax collecting was not looked upon with favor by the Jewish people. A Jewish person employed directly or indirectly by the Romans to collect taxes were hated by their own brethren, who accused them of selling out to foreigners to gain wealth and ease. Tax collectors were like some modern public officials who use the power of their offices to make themselves wealthy. The Pharisees and Scribes considered Jewish tax collectors as apostate (beyond the possibility of repentance). They claimed that if a tax collector could actually repent, he would drop dead immediately to show the sincerity of the repentance!

His Call to Follow Christ

The first three Gospels record this call (see the texts on page 19). It is the view of this author that this call was a call to service, not salvation. If this is correct, then Matthew was converted sometime earlier. Matthew did not immediately leave his job upon his conversion. Sometime later, Jesus approached his tax office and challenged him to follow Him. Jesus had given him time to think about full-time work for the Kingdom. He responded immediately by leaving the employment of the Romans, resolutely leaving all behind (Luke 5:28) and following Christ. How much time elapsed between his conversion and call is not known. However, he must have had some time to consider the cost of stepping out in faith to follow Jesus full-time. It is always wise to count the cost before making any major change in one's life. It is good to remember, too, that when God commands, He also enables. The genuineness of Matthew's step of faith is seen by the big reception he gave Jesus. The purpose of it was to honor the Lord, introduce his friends and associates to Jesus, and publically witness to his new allegiance to Christ (Luke 5:27-29). We should do all three.

> **It is good to remember that when God commands, He also enables.**

His Appointment as an Apostle

Matthew 10:1-4 records the fact that Jesus selected Matthew to be one of the twelve Apostles. He, along with the other eleven, was given special powers to preach and do miracles. The working of miracles served as a sign of the truth of the Gospel message he, and the other Apostles, preached. After many years of preaching, Matthew was inspired by the Holy Spirit to commit the message to written form.

His Humility

This is illustrated by the three Scripture texts. Observe how Matthew is reluctant to say anything that might make him appear to be something special (Matt. 9:9-10). Notice, however, that Mark and Luke give a picture of Matthew which is very commending of his faith and works. The lesson for us should be obvious. It may be summarized in the words of Proverbs 27:2, which reads: "Let another man praise you, and not your own mouth ..."

His Evangelistic Zeal

Matthew had a burden for his lost friends. He gave a great feast, Luke tells us, in honor of Jesus. He made sure that many of his former associates were there so they could meet Jesus and be saved. He was active in evangelism during the Acts period (note the number of times the Apostles are mentioned as a group involved in ministry in Acts). Do we have a burden for the lost like Matthew? To what extent will we go to rescue the perishing? Look at the extent to which God went (John 3:16)!

Matthew, the Book

This magnificent Gospel of 28 chapters stands first in the order of the four Gospels. It begins on a Jewish note—the royal genealogy of Messiah from Abraham and David (1:1-17). It ends on a universal chord—the great commission to go to all the world and preach the Gospel (28:16-20). It starts with the revelation that Messiah would save His people from their sins (1:21), and concludes with the Gospel going out to the nations so that they might be saved as well (28:19-20).

There are many things which could be said in a survey of Matthew, but the following will give us a general grasp of the book.

Date of Writing

When did Matthew put his Gospel into written form? It was probably written somewhere between AD 50 and 70. In AD 70, the city of Jerusalem was totally destroyed by the armies of Rome which were led by General Titus. Jesus, at the end of His ministry, predicted this destruction (22:7; 23:37-38, compared with Luke 21:20-24) which came as a judgment from God because of Israel's rejection of Him. So, when Matthew wrote his Gospel, the fulfillment of Jesus' prediction was yet future. Thus, he had to have written his Gospel before AD 70.

Readers

To whom was this Gospel sent? It seems clear from the standpoint and argument of the book that Matthew wrote primarily to his own Jewish people. First, he constantly quotes from, or alludes to, the Old Testament for the purpose of making or illustrating his point. Secondly, the argument of his book, which he develops in the first 13 chapters and centers around Jesus being the Jewish Messiah, makes sense only if the readers are Jewish.

Portrait of Jesus by Matthew

There is no doubt that Jesus is seen in various roles in Matthew, such as teacher, miracle worker, prophet, and evangelist. However, Messiah-King is the emphasis, and the other roles are supportive in character. Several times in Matthew, Jesus is called the "son of David," and that means royalty. Jesus is the King who came to establish the predicted and long-awaited kingdom.

The Outline Structure of Matthew

Matthew is by far the easiest of the Gospels to outline. His book consists of five discourses and six narratives. The narratives emphasize the *person of Christ* while the discourses stress various aspects of the *messianic kingdom.* Matthew concludes each discourse with words similar to these: "… when Jesus finished these sayings" (7:28; 11:1; 13:53; 19:1; 26:1). Observe the following breakdown based on the narrative-discourse plan:

Narrative	The **Presentation** of the King	1-4
Discourse	The **Principles** of the Kingdom (Sermon on the Mount)	5-7
Narrative	The **Power and Authority** of the King (His miracles)	8-9
Discourse	The **Preachers** of the Kingdom (12 Apostles)	10
Narrative	The **Persecution** of the King	11-12
Discourse	The **Parables** of the Kingdom	13
Narrative	The **Preaching** of the King in Galilee	14-17
Discourse	The **Problem** of Sin in the Kingdom	18
Narrative	The **Preaching** of the King in Judea and Perea	19-23
Discourse	The **Prophecy** Concerning the King (Mt. Olivet Discourse)	24-25
Narrative	The **Passion and Victory** of the King	26-28

The Purpose of Matthew

As mentioned earlier, Matthew's purpose is to demonstrate that the man Jesus is none other than the Messiah-King of the Jews. It is beautiful to see how he develops this.

First, he gives four lines of evidence that Jesus is the true Messiah-King. He follows this with the answers to three crucial questions.

1. The Evidence That Jesus, and Jesus Only, Is Messiah-King

Jesus is *legally* eligible to be the King as the genealogy proves (1:1-17). He is *prophetically* eligible to be the King as proved by six Old Testament prophecies (1:18–3:17). He is *morally* eligible to be the King as seen in His victory over the temptation brought to Him by Satan (4:1-11). He is *ministerially* eligible to be the King as seen by His teaching (5:1–7:29) and miracle ministry (8:1–9:38).

2. Three Crucial Questions Inferred from the First Nine Chapters

Since Jesus is the true Messiah-King of Israel, *did He give a legitimate offer of the kingdom to Israel to whom He was sent*? Chapter 10 clearly shows that He did. He chose twelve Apostles and sent them out telling them that they should go only to the "lost sheep of the house of Israel" (10:5-6). *Was the offer of the kingdom accepted by Israel as a nation*? No! This is illustrated by the nation's rejection of John the Baptist (11:1-30), and Jesus (12:1-50). This poses a serious problem. *If the kingdom message was rejected, what then happens to the unconditional promises of God to establish the kingdom*? The answer is given in the parables of Matthew 13. These parables teach, in part, that the Kingdom in its outward form and manifestation with the King present and ruling is postponed until the second coming of Christ. Nothing can ultimately thwart God's plan to establish His Kingdom in the earth. Jesus shall reign (Ps. 2:6-9; Rev. 11:15).

> **Matthew reminds us in His Gospel that we should have a strategy for reaching the lost. Matthew did.**

An Important Lesson

Matthew's method in demonstrating his purpose for writing his Gospel should remind us that we not only should witness to the identity and purpose of Jesus' coming to the earth, but also have a strategy for reaching the lost. Matthew did. This is easy to see from Matthew 1–13. Do we? Have we formed a plan for reaching the lost ones around us in our neighborhoods, work places, schools, and places of recreation?

THE GOSPEL OF MARK

The Gospel of Mark is small in size but dynamic in message. It is only sixteen chapters long and thus the shortest of the four Gospels. Why so short since the others are much longer? The answer has to do with the original readers–the Romans. They were thinkers, but as a people they were doers rather than thinkers. They were interested in physical accomplishments rather than lengthy and reasoned treatises. In this they are like many in our modern world who have the greatest admiration for people who accomplish great and wonderful feats in sports, music, business, military warfare, education, etc. Their philosophy is, "Let's get to the heart of the matter. Cut away all that is irrelevant. Just show me how it's done and I will do it." We all know people with that kind of mindset, and Mark's Gospel may be the one that will have the most impact on them.

Mark, the Man

The writer of this second Gospel never mentions his name in it, nor is he mentioned by name in any of the other three. He is, however, mentioned in the following texts: Acts 12:12, 25; 13:5, 13; 15:37-39; Colossians 4:10; Philemon 24; 2 Timothy 4:11; 1 Peter 5:13.

His Names

Mark is his Latin name, mentioned ten times in the New Testament, and he is best known by this name. John is his Jewish name. He is called by his combined name, John Mark, three times.

His Background (Acts 12:12-13)

Mark's city was Jerusalem. His mother had a house there in which prayer meetings were held after the church was formed. Two family members are mentioned in the New Testament. There was Mary, his mother, and Barnabas his cousin. Barnabas is mentioned often in Acts. Mark appears to have come from a wealthy background. This inference is based on the fact that his mother's house was big enough to have "many" there for a prayer meeting, and that there were servants in the employ of the household. Mark was probably well educated because of this status.

His Spiritual History—The Making of a Servant of God

Mark was probably a convert to Christ through the Apostle Peter. Why? In 1 Peter 5:13, Peter called him "my son." This probably means son in the faith. Possibly Mark was converted in one of Peter's preaching missions during the early days of the church (Acts 1:1–7:60). Among other things, we are saved to serve, and Mark was committed to labor for Christ. He kept company with Paul and Barnabas (Acts 12:25). The following is an outline of his service.

1. He went with Paul and Barnabas on their first missionary journey (Acts 12:25; 13:5).

2. He was not an equal with Paul and Barnabas as far as the work was concerned. Acts 13:5 classifies him as their "assistant."

3. He left Paul and Barnabas in the middle of the missionary endeavor (Acts 13:13; 15:38). Paul looked upon John Mark's departure from the work as a serious failure.

4. Mark was the object of sharp conflict between Paul and Barnabas, when Barnabas wanted to give him another chance by taking him on the second missionary journey. Paul refused. Who was right, Paul or Barnabas? It has often been said that both were right. Barnabas had the restoration of Mark in view, and Paul had the success of the work at heart. Barnabas did not want John Mark to continue in failure, and Paul did not want the work to be jeopardized (Acts 15:37-39a).

5. Barnabas and Paul split up and Barnabas took John Mark with him. Probably Barnabas, by virtue of his spiritual gift of encouragement, was able to help bring maturity into John Mark's life.

6. Mark did change, for the Apostle Paul speaks well of him some years later while Paul was in prison (Col. 4:10; Philem. 24). Later Paul commended Mark for being useful for the work of service (2 Tim. 4:11).

7. Mark's lasting contribution of service was to write the second Gospel. Though John Mark does not identify himself in his Gospel as its author, the external evidence is very strong for his authorship. It was the early and unanimous opinion of the church that Mark was in company with Peter in Rome during the latter part of Peter's life and that Mark recorded in his Gospel the things which Peter preached about Jesus.

Though Mark does not name himself in his Gospel there is a tradition that he is referring to himself in Mark 14:51. The reasoning is that there is no need to relate this incident of the young man fleeing away naked unless he is in some way related to the producing of the Gospel.

Important Lesson

Mark's experience teaches us that failure does not have to be permanent. We can be restored to the Lord and to the work. If we have fallen, let us take encouragement from Mark's experience, and refocus our minds and our energy, by the power of the Holy Spirit, on what really counts in life. Then let us give ourselves totally to the Lord's service using our spiritual gifts for the good of a lost world and for the benefit of God's people to His everlasting glory.

Mark, the Book

The Brevity of Mark's Gospel

Mark has only 678 verses in its sixteen chapters. That is not much in comparison to the other two synoptic Gospels—Matthew and Luke. The longest Gospel is Luke, having 1,151 verses. Matthew comes next (though having more chapters than Luke) with 1,071 verses. However, we would not want to misjudge the value of Mark on the basis of amount of content. Though brief, Mark is like a pool of pure, clear water, far deeper than it looks.

Omissions

Obviously, if Mark is much shorter, he had to have left out much of Christ's life. For instance, Mark does not record the preliminary ministry of Jesus found in John 1-4. The introductory material of Mark is only thirteen verses long (1:1-13) in comparison to Matthew which has 76 verses, and Luke which has 180. Mark, in other words, does not record the genealogy, the incarnation, the early childhood and three-fold temptation of Jesus. The temptation is mentioned, but not the three tests. The Sermon on the Mount and most of the teaching of Jesus are not mentioned. Mark does say many times that Jesus taught, but does not mention the content of the teaching.

Emphasis and Readers

Mark wanted to emphasize the doing ministry of Jesus. Thus, he mentions 19 miracles in contrast to four parables. This emphasis was no doubt directed by the background of the Romans to whom he wrote. They were a people who gloried in dynamic power and military conquest. They were captivated by deeds, not literary brilliance. So Mark took advantage of his knowledge of what the Romans were like and tailored his story of Christ's life to meet their needs.

As you read through Mark you will be impressed by the fact that the readers of this Gospel lacked certain kinds of background data and understanding of Jewish culture and geography. Mark must explain. You can appreciate this need if you have ever attempted to communicate with someone who is totally foreign to your language and culture. Note some examples:

- *Geography.* The readers were evidently unfamiliar with Palestinian geography so Mark had to explain that the Jordan was a river (1:5); that the Mount of Olives overlooked the Jerusalem temple (13:3), etc.
- *Custom.* Mark informed the Romans that John's disciples and the Pharisees were fasting (2:18).
- *Translation.* Jewish people in Palestine spoke Aramaic so Mark translated some Aramaic expressions so the readers could benefit (3:17; 5:41; 7:34; 14:36; 15:34).
- *Latinism.* Mark inserted some Latin words from time to time. Since there were acceptable Greek equivalents, the readers must have been Roman in background.

Portrait of Jesus—The Servant of God

Mark's presentation of Jesus is exactly the opposite of Matthew's. Matthew, you will remember, presented Jesus as the Messiah-King before whom all must bow in submission and allegiance. Mark, on the other hand, presented Jesus in the role of a servant who was totally submissive to the Father's will. The key verse supporting this portrait is Mark 10:45: "For even the Son of Man came not to be served but to serve, and to give His life as a ransom for many."

The background of this presentation of Christ is the many servant passages found in the Old Testament book of Isaiah. There the term "my servant" is used several times, sometimes referring to the nation of Israel and at other times prophetically of the Messiah, Jesus Christ (Isaiah 42:1-4; 49:6; 52:13; 53:11). The Apostle Paul also emphasized the servant role of Jesus in Philippians 2:5-11. In a sense, Mark 10:45 forms the basis for the general outline structure of Mark as one observes it as follows.

Outline Structure of Mark

1. *The Servant Introduced (1:1-13).* These thirteen verses introduce the servant as the Son of God who was proclaimed and baptized by John the Baptist. The temptation by Satan followed.
2. *The Servant Serving (1:14–10:52).* These chapters show Him serving in Galilee, north of Galilee and in Judea. They illustrate that He came not to be served, but to serve.
3. *The Servant Suffering (11:1–15:47).* These chapters emphasize the passion week and they record the fact that Jesus gave His life a ransom for many.
4. *The Servant Victorious (16:1-20).* The evidence of this victory was the bodily resurrection of Jesus from the dead, His appearance to various believers, and His commission to the Apostles to preach the Gospel to all the world.

Mark's Style of Writing

Some books are ponderous because they are wordy and drawn out due to emphasizing detail. These take time and effort to read and digest. Others are brief, to the point, and fast-reading. Mark is like the latter category. His style is concise, fast-moving, and sometimes breathless. One illustration of this is a word he used 42 times (*euthus* in the Greek language) which in the old KJV is rendered by five different English words: "straightway ... immediately ... forthwith ... as soon as ... anon." The New American Standard version always translates *euthus* by the word "immediately." The New King James in most instances uses "immediately." Read Mark 1:9-45 where "immediately" is used several times and you will sense the fast-moving drama of Christ at work doing the Father's will. As a servant he was always on the move, always ministering to the needs of others, always showing His great power. As we have said, this would greatly appeal to the Romans or anyone who has a mind to work and accomplish things. All believers ought to have this kind of servant mindset. We have been called to serve our great God. Are we doing it, or simply living for ourselves? Let us refresh our memories with the principles Jesus taught us to live by so that we might be successful servants in the Kingdom. What are these? (l) We should deny ourselves, (2) take up the cross and (3) follow Christ (Mark 8:34-38).

> **We should deny ourselves, take up the cross, and follow Christ.**

THE GOSPEL OF LUKE

Luke, the Man

God used a variety of men to write the New Testament books. He used a tax collector (Matthew), a wealthy young man (Mark), fishermen (Peter and John), a Rabbi (Paul), two half-brothers of Jesus (James and Jude) and last, but not least, Luke. Paul wrote more books of the New Testament than Luke, but Luke's two volumes (his Gospel and the book of Acts) when put together are longer than all the writings of Paul. What do we know about this man?

His Racial Background

Luke was the only Gentile writer of the New Testament. How do we know he was a Gentile? We know by comparing the names mentioned in Colossians 4:7-14. All the names from verse seven through verse eleven are Jewish ("of the circumcision"). Those mentioned in verses 12-14 (of which Luke is one) are Gentiles.

His Occupation

Luke was a medical doctor. Colossians 4:14 is the only reference which attests to this occupation. In support of this, Luke used a lot of medical terminology in his Gospel. As well, Luke looks at the miracles of Jesus from a doctor's point of view. Compare the story of the healing of a leper as found in the synoptic Gospels (Luke 5:12; Mark 1:40; Matt. 8:2). Matthew and Mark simply say he was a leper, whereas Luke describes him as "a man *full* of leprosy."

His Intellectual Ability

We usually think of medical doctors as very intelligent people. Luke's intelligence is witnessed by his large vocabulary, his writing ability, and the very sophisticated preface (1:1-4) to his book. The New Testament was written in the common Greek of the day, but Luke wrote his preface in classical Greek which shows he was very well educated and scholarly.

His Association with the Apostle Paul

Paul viewed Luke as one of his best friends. Note how Paul describes him:

- He called him "the beloved physician" (Col. 4:14). "Beloved" is a special term of endearment, someone who is very special. We may love many people but only a few are beloved.
- He called him a "fellow worker" (Philem. 24). Luke travelled with Paul on many of his missionary journeys helping out in the ministry of the Gospel (see the "we" sections of the book of Acts where Luke shows his personal involvement with Paul: Acts 16:10; 20:5-6; 21:15; 27:1; 28:16).
- Paul relates in his second Roman imprisonment that "Luke alone is with me." (2 Tim. 4:11). Paul in this imprisonment was facing execution. Luke was a faithful friend to the very end of Paul's life, never allowing severe adversity to cause disloyalty to him.

Luke, the Book

The Readers

Luke wrote directly to a Greek whom he called "most excellent Theophilus" (1:3), and through Theophilus to the Greek world. The Greeks were interested in producing a perfect human being. Luke is saying in his Gospel that the Greeks need search no longer. In Jesus Christ he has been found. Twenty-six times in his Gospel, Luke calls Jesus "the Son of Man." This emphasizes Jesus' humanity. Jesus is the perfect and true representative of humanity. There has never been, and never will be, another person like Jesus Christ. Paul exclaimed, "Great indeed…is the mystery of godliness: He was manifested in the flesh" (1 Tim. 3:16).

Background for Writing the Gospel of Luke (1:1-4)

We know next to nothing about Theophilus. His name means "lover of God." Luke addressed him as "most excellent." This is a title of high governmental officials or of the wealthy class (see Acts 23:26; 26:25). Theophilus had been instructed in the truth of Christianity and Luke, through his Gospel, wants to convey to Theophilus the certainty of what he had learned.

Luke told Theophilus that many had attempted to write the life story of Jesus and that he was motivated to write an account as well. He assured him that he had employed intense research of all available materials with the greatest caution. Of course, the Holy Spirit was guiding him in his research. Bible scholars believe that Luke compiled his materials for his Gospel during the two years (AD 56–58) Paul was in prison in Caesarea (Acts 23:23–26:32) and wrote it about AD 59.

The Scope of Luke's Gospel

Luke begins with the angelic announcement of the births of John the Baptist and Jesus (1:1–2:52), and thus starts earlier than Matthew and Mark. It ends with the ascension of Jesus to heaven (24:50-53). Remember it is the longest of the Gospels.

The General Outline Structure of Luke

1. *Introduction—First Advent of the Son of Man (1:1–4:13).* Chapters 1–2 give the birth stories of John and Jesus and are unique to Luke. Chapters 3:1–4:13 record the preparation (baptism, temptation, etc.) of Jesus for His ministry, which Matthew and Mark also record.

2. *The Ministry of the Son of Man in Galilee (4:14–9:50).* The content of these chapters is basically what Matthew and Mark record of the Galilean ministry of Jesus. Luke, of course, writes it from his own perspective. Jesus was popular in Galilee with the common people.

3. *The Ministry of the Son of Man in Judea-Perea (9:51–19:27).* The majority of this content is unique to Luke. It contains a lot of the teaching ministry of Jesus not found in the other Gospels.

4. *The Ministry of the Son of Man in Jerusalem (19:28–24:53).* This section records the passion-week ministry of Jesus in which He gave His life as our sacrifice for sin upon the cross. It records His burial, resurrection, and post-resurrection ministry.

The Universal Nature of Luke's Gospel

Luke makes it clear that the Gospel is for all mankind and that Jesus is the Savior of the world. Luke begins with the angelic message that the good news is "to all people" (2:10; see also 2:14), and it ends with the Lord's commission to the apostles that "repentance for the forgiveness of sins should be proclaimed in His name to all nations" (24:47). John the Baptist preached that "all flesh shall see the salvation of God" (3:4-6). Even Samaritans can be saved (9:54; 10:33; 17:16); they were a mixed race despised by the Jewish people (compare

> **Luke makes it clear that the Gospel is for all mankind and that Jesus is the Savior of the world.**

John 4). The word "salvation" with its various forms (save, saved) is a favorite of Luke's and is used 20 times by him. A key verse of Luke is 19:10: "for the Son of Man came to seek and to save the lost."

Some of the Special Interests of Luke

Luke has a special interest in the *parable ministry of Jesus*. He records 22 of these. Of the 22 parables, 17 are found only in Luke. Most of the parables he records center in people.

He has a special interest in the *miracle ministry of Jesus*. He records 20 miracles and all but six are given elsewhere. The miracles are in the context of being acts of compassion as well as being signs of Christ's person and identity.

He has a special interest in the *prayer life of Jesus*. He records ten episodes of prayer in the life of our Lord (3:21; 5:15-16; 6:12; 9:18-22; 9:29; 10:21; 11:1; 22:39-46; 23:34; 23:46). Eight of these episodes are found only in Luke. All of them are associated with some important event. Two of Luke's parables deal with teaching on prayer.

One of Luke's biggest special interests is *people*. He focuses on both individuals and groups. He loved social outcasts (7:36-50; 10:30-42; 15:11-32; 19:1-10; 23:39-43). He cared about infants, children and young people (1:1–2:52; 7:12; 8:31; 9:38).

A fifth special interest was *social relationships* (15:1). There are six dining episodes in Luke. Three of these were with Christ's enemies (7:36-50; 11:37-44; 14:1-4) and three with His friends (10:38-43; 19:1-10; 24:13-32).

Last but not least is the special interest Luke had in *women*. Luke mentions women 43 times (more than the other three Gospels put together). Thirteen of the women are not mentioned elsewhere and two of them are the subjects of parables (Luke 15; 18). Women helped to support Christ's ministry (8:1-3).

The Holy Spirit in Luke's Gospel

Luke is very interested in the person and work of the Holy Spirit. He mentions the Holy Spirit 18 times in his Gospel and 57 times in the book of Acts for a total of 75 times. He teaches that the Holy Spirit is a distinct person of the Trinity (see Luke 3:22 where all three persons of the Trinity are distinguished), and he teaches that the Holy Spirit is truly God in Acts 5:3-4 (compare lying to the Holy Spirit and lying to God). However, the big emphasis on the Spirit in Luke's writings is on the work of the Spirit–what the Spirit does to and through His servants (such as filling and baptizing). In his Gospel, Luke speaks of the Holy Spirit in relation to both Christ and His followers. Some references concerning the Holy Spirit and Christ are Luke 3:22; 4:1. Some references concerning the Holy Spirit and believers are Luke 1:15, 35, 41, 67 and 2:26-27.

Important Lesson from Luke

Luke is careful to point out that Jesus Christ is not only the Son of God (1:35), but He is also man. Jesus Christ is unique. He is one person with two natures. A mere human is one person and one nature, but Jesus Christ is fully God and fully man. As man, Dr. Luke points out that "the child grew and became strong, filled with wisdom. And the favor of God was upon Him.... And Jesus increased in wisdom and in stature and in favor with God and man" (2:40, 52). This is a great mystery which we cannot fully understand (1 Tim. 3:16) and should not attempt to rationalize. Through church history some have erred in both directions, of either denying His full deity or genuine humanity. Cults are especially in error over the person of Christ. Hold fast to the truth of the Bible about Christ's person. He is fully God and fully man!

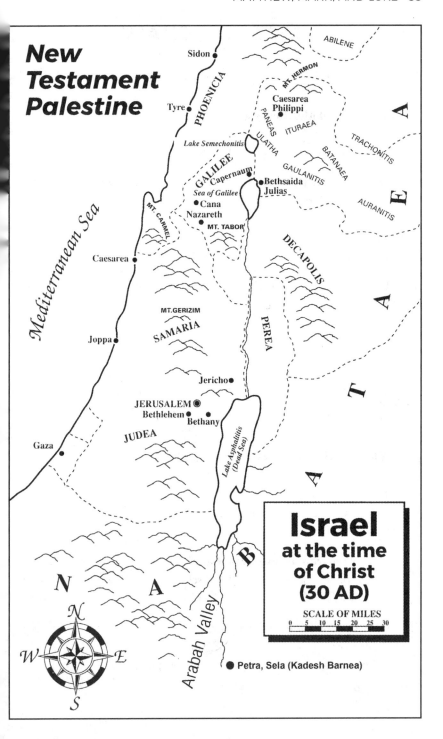

New Testament Palestine

Israel at the time of Christ (30 AD)

SCALE OF MILES
0 5 10 15 20 25 30

Petra, Sela (Kadesh Barnea)

LESSON 2 EXAM

Use the exam sheet at the back of the book to complete your exam.

1. **Jesus' call of Matthew was a call to**
   A. salvation.
   B. sanctification.
   C. serenity.
   D. service.

2. **Matthew's portrait of Jesus in his Gospel is that of the**
   A. Son of God.
   B. devoted servant.
   C. Messiah-King.
   D. Son of Man.

3. **The outline structure of Matthew consists of**
   A. five discourses and six narratives.
   B. 14 chapters of history and 14 of prophecy.
   C. narrative, parables, prophecy.
   D. none of the above.

4. **Mark was probably a convert to Christ through**
   A. Peter.
   B. Paul.
   C. Barnabas.
   D. James.

5. **When Mark wrote his Gospel he omitted the**
   A. genealogy of Christ.
   B. incarnation of Christ.
   C. the early childhood of Jesus.
   D. all of the above.

6. **Mark's portrait of Jesus was that of a**
   A. prophet.
   B. priest.
   C. servant.
   D. king.

7. **Luke's occupation was that of a**
   A. lawyer.
   B. business man.
   C. medical doctor.
   D. philosopher.

8. **Luke presented Jesus to the Greek world as the**
   A. Son of God.   C. Son of the Father.
   B. Son of Man.   D. Son of the Jews.

9. **Luke is the only Gospel writer to record**
   A. the baptism of Jesus.
   B. the birth stories of John and Jesus.
   C. the temptation in the wilderness.
   D. the parables of Jesus.

10. **In Luke's writings, he emphasizes the Spirit's**
    A. person.   C. wisdom.
    B. work.   D. guidance.

What Do You Say?

Is the fact that Matthew presents Jesus as the promised Messiah significant to us today? Why?

_____

_____

_____

_____

John and Acts

THE GOSPEL OF JOHN

In regards to literary style, the Gospel of John is quite plain in comparison to the Synoptic Gospels. Its vocabulary is the most limited of the four Gospels and its sentence structure is quite simple. This is why I advise new believers in Christ to make it their first reading in the New Testament. However, with all John's simplicity, many Bible scholars point out that John is the most theologically profound book of the four Gospels. So God took a theologically uneducated fisherman (Acts 4:13) and conveyed through his simple vocabulary some of the most deep and profound truths concerning Jesus, the Son of God. Let us get to know this man who was chosen to write the fourth Gospel.

> **The book of John is the most theologically profound book of the four Gospels.**

John, the Man

His Name

The parents of John, Mr. and Mrs. Zebedee, must have been touched by God's grace, because when their son was born they called him John which means "the LORD is gracious." John may not have been impressed by his name as he was growing up, but he certainly must have seen its significance after he came to know Jesus and committed himself to Him.

His Family

His father, Zebedee, was a fisherman, and John, along with his brother James, was in the fishing business too (Matt. 4:21). In fact, it was while he was engaged in this employment that Jesus challenged him to devote his full time to the Kingdom. Christ would make John (and his brother James) a "fisher of men."

His Negative Characteristics

There are three passages in the New Testament Gospels which show that John had a lot to learn. First, he shows a very narrow and exclusive spirit in Mark 9:38. He and his brother saw someone casting out demons in Christ's name and they tried to stop him because he was not following them. Jesus taught John through this incident that the person who is not against them is actually for them (Mark 9:39). Secondly, John (and his brother James) showed a very strong, revengeful spirit as they traveled toward Jerusalem. A city in the province of Samaria would not receive Jesus (Luke 9:51-53). This greatly angered John and James and they asked Jesus if He wanted them to call down fire from heaven and consume them (Luke 9:54). Jesus rebuked them and reminded them that He came to save people not destroy them (Luke 9:55-56). Thirdly, the spirit of selfishness is seen in John and James as they seek to be enthroned with Jesus on His left and right hand in the Kingdom. Matthew 20:20-28 shows the mother of James and John making the request, and Mark 10:35-45 pictures the young men making it. There is no contradiction. The two accounts when seen together give us the whole truth—that both mother and sons were desirous of this favor. Jesus countered this lust for greatness by showing that the essence of greatness is in being a servant (Mark 10:43-44), and that this had been His own example to them (Mark 10:45).

His Call

John was first called to be a "fisher of men" (Matt. 4:18-22) and then sometime later he was called, along with eleven others, to be an Apostle (Mark 3:13-19). Mark 3:13-15 tells us that "He (Jesus) appointed twelve (whom he also named apostles) so that they might be with Him and He might send them out to preach and have authority to cast out demons." He became one of the leading Apostles along with Peter in the first twelve chapters of Acts.

His Writings

John wrote five of the New Testament books (John's Gospel, 1 John, 2 John, 3 John and Revelation). In reading these five books, one discerns that he overcame the three negative characteristics mentioned previously. His narrow, revengeful, selfish spirit was replaced by a vision for the salvation of the world, love for all, and a selfless spirit. We all need to grow, to replace the negative things in our lives that hinder us and others. John especially emphasizes this in 1 John.

John, the Book

Authorship

The author of this Gospel never introduces himself by the name "John" or identifies himself as an Apostle. He does identify himself a number of times as the disciple whom Jesus loved (13:23; 18:15-16; 19:26-27). Evangelical scholars tell us that since the beginning of the second century it has been the constant testimony of the church that the Apostle John, son of Zebedee, wrote this Gospel. Support for this is very detailed, involved, and beyond the scope of this course. It is clear from the content of John that the author (1) was a Jewish person, (2) lived in Palestine, (3) an eyewitness of the life and ministry of Jesus, and (4) was John the Apostle. The arguments which evangelical scholars put forth to support these four points, though too lengthy to include here, are both clear and convincing.

> **Jesus is not only King, Servant, and Perfect Man, *He is God*.**

In terms of time, John wrote his Gospel several years after the Synoptic Gospels were written. Scholars date it somewhere between AD 85–95.

The Outline Structure of John's Gospel

1. *The Prelude to the Life and Ministry of the Son of God (1:1-18)*. "In the beginning was the Word, and the Word was with God, and the Word was God. He was in the beginning with God" (1:1-2). In this way this majestic prelude to John's Gospel begins. It emphasizes the fourth portrait of the Gospels. Jesus is not only King, Servant, and Perfect Man, *He is God* ("and the Word was God"). This One who is called "the Word" is further identified as the Creator (1:3), the Life (1:4), the Light (1:4-9), and the One

who became the incarnate Son of God (1:14). Jesus, the Son of God, came to His own people but they did not receive him, "But to all who did receive Him, who believed in His name, He gave the right to become children of God" (1:12). Have you received Jesus as your personal Savior?

2. *The Public Ministry of the Son of God to the World (1:19–12:50).* Jesus was concerned that men and women come to Him for salvation. In these chapters we see Him taking the initiative and extending Himself to the spiritually lost and dying. We find Him ministering to individuals (like Nicodemus, chapter 3) and groups (like the 5,000 He fed, chapter 6). It is very educational to observe the evangelistic methods He used to meet the needs of others. We can use these methods, too, in our own witness.

> **To all who receive Jesus, who believe in His name, He gives the right to become children of God.**

3. *The Private Ministry of the Son of God to His Own (13:1–17:26).* These chapters have been traditionally called the Upper Room Discourse. On the night Jesus was betrayed by Judas, He met with His Apostles in a private dwelling to celebrate the Passover. Jesus took advantage of this occasion to teach His Apostles many important things for them to know in the light of the fact that He was going back to heaven to the Father. Some of these teachings (such as love, humility, faith, second coming, Holy Spirit, etc.) are expanded on later in Acts and the Epistles. Jesus also prayed for their unity and preservation (17).

4. *The Passion and Resurrection of the Son of God (18:1–21:25).* All the Gospels record our Lord's trials, sufferings, death, and resurrection. Understandably, this is the major focus of the Gospel records because of the reason for the Son of God's coming to earth. After Christ's resurrection, He appeared to some of His followers. Peter was a special focus of our Lord's attention (21:15-25) for he was in need of restoration to Christ's service. Peter benefited from the Lord's confrontation ("do you love Me," 21:15-17) and became a spiritual and courageous servant as Acts 1–12 bear witness.

John's Portrait of Jesus—He Is God!

Observe the following evidence in John's Gospel which proves Christ's deity (that He was indeed God).

- The statements made in the Prelude which we have already mentioned and to which you may refer (1:1).
- Jesus claimed to be God, and those who heard Him make this claim understood Him to be making it, and they sought to kill Him (5:17-18; 8:58; 10:30-38).
- Thomas, after the resurrection of Jesus, made his famous confession to Jesus recognizing His deity, "My Lord and My God" (20:28).
- When John gave his purpose for writing his Gospel (20:30-31) he gave witness to Christ's deity by saying that the sign-miracles Jesus did were for the purpose of showing that "He is the Christ, the Son of God ..." Eight of these sign miracles are recorded in John.
- The "I AM" statements of Jesus all point to His deity. There are two categories. First, there are the seven "I AMs" with a predicate: "I am the bread of life ... light ... door ... good shepherd ... resurrection and the life ... the way, truth and life ... and the true vine" (6:35; 8:12; 10:7, 9; 10:11; 11:25; 14:6; 15:1). The second category is the "I AMs" without a predicate (nothing follows the verb "am"). That is where Jesus simply says that He is *the* "I AM." There are seven of these as well (4:26; 8:24, 28, 58; 13:19; 18:5, 8). These "I AMs" without predicates identify Jesus with the "I AM" (Jehovah) of the Old Testament (Ex. 3:13-14), easily demonstrating Christ's deity.

The Uniqueness of John's Gospel

Scholars point out that approximately ninety percent of John's Gospel is not found in the other three. For instance, the preliminary ministry of Jesus (John 1-4) is not found elsewhere. All the discourses of Jesus found in John are not given elsewhere (5-11 and 13-17). Six of the eight miracles in John are not given elsewhere: water into wine (2), Nobleman's son healed (4), impotent man healed (5), blind man received sight (9), the raising of Lazarus (11), and providing fish (21). The other two—feeding of the 5,000 and Jesus walking on the water (6)—are found in the Synoptic Gospels.

Another aspect of uniqueness is the distribution of content. There are 879 verses in John and 648 of these have to do with the Judean ministry of Jesus. The rest (231 verses) cover Christ's ministry in Galilee, Perea, and Samaria. Thus, if we did not have John's Gospel we would be without a lot of knowledge of the ministry of Jesus. Obviously, John's focus in his Gospel is on the Judean ministry. The distribution of content is also interesting in terms of time. John's Gospel covers about three and one-half years of time. In fact, it is from John's Gospel that we learn that Jesus' ministered for over three years. How is this determined? It is figured on the basis of the number of mentions of the Jewish feast of the Passover. The Passover is mentioned three times by name (2:13; 6:4; 11:55) and once without name (5:1). So from 2:13 to 5:1 is one year. Then 5:1 to 6:4 is a second year. Finally, 6:4 to 11:55 is the third year. Since John 1:1-2:12 covers about six months, the total time coverage of John is three and one-half years. The distribution of content in terms of time works out as follows:

- Three-quarters of John (7-21) took place in the last six months of the ministry of Jesus.
- Approximately one-half of John (12:12-20:31) took place in the passion week at Jerusalem.
- Approximately one-third of John (13-19) took place in less than a 24-hour period.

The Holy Spirit in John's Gospel

John, like Luke, is interested in the Holy Spirit. He mentions the Holy Spirit in relation to Christ seven times (1:32, 33; 3:34; 15:26-twice; 16:7, 14). Jesus said that He must go away before the Spirit would come and begin a new age (16:7).

John shows the ministry the Holy Spirit would have to the unbelieving world. When the Spirit comes, Jesus said He would convict the world of sin, righteousness, and judgment (16:7-11). This ministry of the Spirit has been going on for 2,000 years!

To the believer, John taught that the Holy Spirit would give new life (3:5-6), be a helper (14:16), teacher (14:26), giver of revelation (16:13-15), and be a refreshment and blessing (7:39).

John taught that the Holy Spirit would be with them and that after Pentecost He would be in them (14:17). On Pentecost (Acts 2:1-13) the Spirit came to indwell the church and empower it to proclaim the Gospel throughout the earth (Acts 1:8).

Favorite Words of John

John's favorite words are *love, father, light, life, believe,* and *witness.* He uses the word *believe* 98 times and looks upon it as the only condition for salvation. He uses the word *witness* (combining noun and verb) 47 times. The Synoptic Gospels together use this word only 16 times making John preeminently the Gospel of Witness. A practical thing to remember is that someone witnessed to us at one point in our life and we believed. We have the responsibility to give witness to the person and work of Jesus Christ so that others can have the same salvation we received (compare Rom. 10:14-15).

THE ACTS OF THE APOSTLES

Acts is the church on the move–empowered by the Holy Spirit, unified, caring for one another, preaching the Gospel, souls being saved, churches established, withstanding persecution, making its influence felt throughout the Roman Empire. What a great book it is—challenging our faith, encouraging our hope, inspiring our love for Christ, for one another and for the world for which Christ died (John 3:16). Believers should read it often so as to remind themselves that God's work done in the power of the Holy Spirit will not come short of His blessing and success.

The Author of Acts

Luke, the "beloved physician" and very capable historian, not only contributed to the New Testament his wonderful and captivating Gospel, but he also wrote the Acts of the Apostles. As inferred by comparing Acts 1:1 with Luke 1:1-4, Luke continues the story of Christianity in Acts: "In the first book [Luke's Gospel], O Theophilus, I have dealt with all that Jesus began to do and teach, until the day when He was taken up, after He had given commands through the Holy Spirit to the apostles whom He had chosen" (Acts 1:1-2). So Luke will begin his ongoing story of Christianity in Acts where he leaves off in his Gospel (Luke 24)—Christ's appearance to His own and His ascension to heaven. Conservatives date the writing of Acts sometime during Paul's two-year imprisonment in Rome (Acts 28:30)—about AD 59–61.

The Importance of Acts

Think about it! Suppose we did not have the book of Acts in the canon of New Testament books. If we did not have Acts, we would lack very important and vital information on the continuing history of Christianity. Among other things, (1) we would not know about the choosing of a new Apostle to take the place of Judas; (2) we would not know about the arrival of the Holy Spirit and His powerful ministry in and through believers; (3) we would not know about the formation of the church on the day of Pentecost (predicted by Jesus); (4) we would not know about the missionary ministry of Peter (Acts 1–12) and Paul (Acts 13–28); (5) we would not know about the dynamic spread of the Gospel from Jerusalem to Rome; (6) we would not know about the persecution of the early church; (7) we would not have the many biographical sketches of people not mentioned elsewhere in the New Testament; and (8) we would not have the historic background for the writing of many of Paul's letters to the churches he established under God. Truly, Acts is a bridge between the Gospels and the Epistles and without this history we would not only be very poor in terms of our knowledge and understanding of the establishment of the early church, but much of what Paul wrote in his letters would be a mystery. Make it one of your goals in the study of the Bible to know this book well. Read it and re-read it. Master its content and development, and it will greatly aid you in interpreting many of Paul's letters.

> If we did not have Acts, we would lack very important and vital information on the continuing history of Christianity.

The Title of Acts

At the head of Acts 1 in most English Bibles is the title, "The Acts of the Apostles." This title has been unduly criticized by some Bible commentaries as inadequate in terms of description of the content of the book. Since only two of the original Apostles, Peter and John, are highlighted in Acts, and since the book emphasizes the Holy Spirit's ministry, why should it be called by this title? In answer to this criticism, the Apostles as a group, in ministering, are mentioned several times (2:43; 4:33; 5:12, 29, 40; 6:2, 6, etc.), and the title as we have it does not in any way deny the ministry of the Holy Spirit through them.

The Structure of Acts

Is there any discernible literary arrangement followed by Luke? Yes. The general movement of Acts is based on its key verse, Acts 1:8: "But you will receive power when the Holy Spirit has come upon you; and you will be witnesses to Me in Jerusalem, and in all Judea and Samaria, and to the end of the earth." It is very easy to see this geographic pattern of Gospel witness as Acts proceeds. The ultimate goal of witness is "to the end of the earth," but Luke's plan, guided by the Holy Spirit, was to record the history of the early church ending with Paul's two-year imprisonment in Rome. The modern day believer must continue to fulfill the commission "to the end of the earth" and can be assured that the power of the Holy Spirit experienced by the early Christians is available to accomplish this task.

There are several success-indicators in the book of Acts to encourage the reader that God was greatly working through His witnesses (6:7; 9:31; 12:24-25; 16:5; 19:20; 28:30-31) to fulfill His will in evangelism. These summaries emphasize the spreading of the Word, the salvation of souls, the building up of the church, etc. These are all things God is continuing to do throughout the world today even in the midst of poverty in some areas and persecution in others.

For the purpose of this survey of Acts the following general outline of the book should be sufficient:

1. The Preaching of the Gospel in Jerusalem—The Ministry of Peter (1:1–6:7)

Introduction (1:1-26)

This chapter begins where the Gospels finish—the post-resurrection appearances of Christ, the great commission to spread the Gospel and the ascension of Christ (1:10-11). It continues with Peter's explanation of the apostasy of Judas and the choice of a new Apostle to take his place—Matthias (1:12-26). So the Apostles and many disciples wait in Jerusalem for the arrival of the Holy Spirit to empower them to fulfill the great commission (1:4-8).

The Arrival of the Holy Spirit to Form and Empower the Church (2:1-47)

Jesus had promised the coming of the Spirit and now He suddenly arrived to God's waiting people to baptize and fill them. It was the day of Pentecost and Jewish people from various parts of the empire were in Jerusalem to celebrate this feast. Believers began to speak the message of

God in the languages of these foreign Jewish people. The Jewish visitors were amazed that these simple Galileans were speaking God's truth in their own languages. How could this be? What does it all mean? Peter, God's man of the hour, was ready to give the answer. A new age had dawned and the central and dominating figure of that age was Jesus Christ. Peter preached the person and work of Christ and called upon all to repent and believe the Gospel. Thousands did just that and the church was born that day. The converts were baptized in water and "devoted themselves to the apostles' teaching and the fellowship, to the breaking of bread and the prayers" (Acts 2:42).

The Earliest Days of the Church in Jerusalem (3:1–6:7)

Peter continued his preaching ministry and thousands more believed the Gospel and were saved. Persecution from the Jewish leaders was brought against Peter and John in Acts 4 and against all the Apostles in Acts 5. This, however, did not stop them. They rejoiced that they were counted worthy to suffer for Christ. A practical problem concerning the distribution of goods to widows (6:1-6) was solved by the appointment of seven spiritual men to handle it, and then Luke closes this section by his first success-indicator: "The Word of God continued to increase, and the number of the disciples multiplied greatly in Jerusalem, and a great many of the priests became obedient to the faith" (Acts 6:7).

2. Critical Events in the Lives of Three Key Figures (6:8–9:31)

The focus is now switching from Jerusalem to Judea and Samaria. Three outstanding men are brought before us in this major section of Acts. The first is Stephen (6:8–7:60) who became the first Christian martyr. The second is Phillip the evangelist who ministered in Samaria (8:4-40) and saw many Samaritans become saved. The third is the Apostle Paul who started a persecution against believers (8:1-3), but then became the most ardent follower of Christ after his conversion on the Damascus road (9:1-31). The risen Christ told Ananias (9:15-16) that Paul was to be "a chosen instrument of mine to carry my name before the Gentiles and kings and the children of Israel. For I will show him how much he must suffer for the sake of my name." Paul's ministry is recorded by Luke in Acts 13–28. Luke closes this section by his second success-indicator: "Then the churches throughout all Judea, Galilee, and Samaria had peace and were edified. And walking in the fear of the Lord and in the comfort of the Holy Spirit, they were multiplied" (9:31). After this important transitional section of three pivotal figures (Stephen, Philip, and Paul), the narrative returns to its chief emphasis—the ministry of Peter.

3. The Ministry of Peter Continued (9:32–12:25)

This section finds Peter traveling in Palestine in fulfillment of his Apostolic mission. He healed Aeneas (9:32-35), restored Dorcas to life (9:36-43) and preached the Gospel in the household of a Gentile Roman soldier by the name of Cornelius, where many were saved and baptized with the Holy Spirit (10:1–11:18). The story of Cornelius is very important because it demonstrates God's intention to make no distinctions between Jewish people and Gentiles in terms of salvation and position in the church. All believers of whatever background are brought into the body of Christ—the church—on the same basis—faith in Jesus Christ. There are no second class citizens in the church (see Eph. 2–3).

Luke makes a slight digression from Peter in Acts 11:19-30 to show the success that other believers were having in evangelism among Jewish people in Phoenicia, Cyprus, and Antioch of Syria. This good news reached Jerusalem, and Barnabas was appointed to observe the work in Antioch. He was thrilled with what he saw and so went to Tarsus to get Paul so that they might return to Antioch and minister there. It was in Antioch that believers were first called Christians. Paul and Barnabas taught the assembly in Antioch for a whole year and then went on an errand of mercy to Jerusalem. Now the narrative returns to Peter in chapter 12.

> **Persecution cannot stop the church. Jesus predicted that "the gates of hell shall not prevail against it."**

Herod Agrippa I (AD 37–44) was ruling Palestine. He had James the Apostle put to death (12:1-4), and seeing that it pleased the Jewish crowds, he arrested Peter and put him in prison. The church prayed for him and God used an angel to miraculously deliver him (12:5-10). Peter went immediately to the brethren, told them what happened (12:11-17) and departed Jerusalem. Herod had the Roman guard put to death and then he went to Caesarea where God punished him with death (12:18-23). Luke ends this major section by once again giving us one of his success-indicators: "But the word of God increased and multiplied" (12:24). Persecution cannot stop the church. Jesus predicted that "the gates of hell shall not prevail against it" (Matt. 16:18).

4. The Ministry of the Apostle Paul (13:1–28:31)

The focus of the book of Acts shifts from Jerusalem to Antioch, from Peter to Paul, from evangelizing the Jewish people to evangelizing the Gentiles. The scene is Antioch in Syria where the church is meeting, ministering to the Lord, and fasting. The Holy Spirit spoke: "'Set apart for me Barnabas and Saul for the work to which I have called them.' Then after fasting and praying they laid their hands on them and sent them off" (13:2-3). Thus begins the dynamic missionary program of Paul, the Apostle who will carry the Gospel to the regions beyond the borders of Palestine. This part of the book of Acts easily falls into five sections as follows:

The First Missionary Journey of Paul (13:1–14:28)

After being commissioned to the work, along with Barnabas (John Mark also traveling with them as a helper), the missionary team sailed from Seleucia (the port city of Antioch) to the island of Cyprus (13:4-13). From Cyprus they sailed north to what we know today as Turkey. There Paul preached in Antioch of Pisidia (13:14-52), Iconium (14:1-5), Lystra (14:6-20), and Derbe (14:21a). Many were saved and the missionary team returned through Lystra, Iconium, and Antioch to encourage and strengthen these new believers in the faith. Elders were appointed in every church and, before they sailed back to Antioch in Syria, they preached in Perga. Arriving back in Antioch they gave their missionary report of all that God had done. They particularly emphasized that God had opened the door of faith to the Gentiles (14:21b-28). It was to these new churches that the Apostle Paul sometime later sent his epistle to the Galatians.

Paul's method of operation during this journey was to go to the synagogue and minister there. Upon being rejected he turned to the Gentiles who accepted the Gospel readily and in great numbers. This made the Jewish listeners very jealous and opposing (13:14-52). Other negatives on the journey were satanic opposition (13:6-11), the departure of John Mark from the work (13:13), and the stoning of Paul in Lystra (14:19-20). When doing the work of God sincerely and with zeal, the believer can expect some opposition from the world and Satan. Sometimes the difficulties come from those believers who are working beside you in the church!

The Jerusalem Council (15:1-35)

Before Paul proceeded on his second missionary journey a council convened in Jerusalem for the purpose of handling a serious doctrinal

Paul's First Missionary Journey

problem dealing with the relationship of Jewish circumcision to salvation. Peter, Paul, Barnabas and James addressed the assembled group and it was determined that Gentiles did not have to be circumcised to be saved. This decree, along with other items, was sent to the Gentile churches. Unfortunately there are groups today that still do not understand that works and ritual have nothing to do with salvation (Eph. 2:8-9).

The Second Missionary Journey of Paul (15:36–18:22)

A controversy arose between Paul and Barnabas concerning John Mark. Barnabas wanted to take him along on the second missionary journey and Paul refused. Paul prevailed and so he and Barnabas parted company. Barnabas took Mark to Cyprus, and Paul chose Silas to take his place (15:36-41). They visited some of the churches started on the first missionary journey and obtained a young man, Timothy, from the area of Lystra and Derbe to go along with them. Timothy turned out to be one of Paul's most trusted associates (16:1-5). At this point in Acts, Luke gives his fourth success-indicator: "So the churches were strengthened in the faith, and they increased in numbers daily" (16:5).

Paul's Second Missionary Journey

Luke's historical emphasis in the second journey is on Europe. He points out that the Holy Spirit prevented the missionary team from preaching in certain places (16:6-8). At Troas, where Luke joined the team (notice "we" in 16:10), Paul received a vision in which a man of Macedonia called him to "come over to Macedonia and help us." Paul obeyed the message of the vision and embarked on his European campaign. God greatly blessed this effort (though there was suffering and persecution) with the salvation of souls and the establishment of churches. Paul preached in Philippi (16:6-40), Thessalonica (17:1-9), Berea (17:10-14), Athens (17:15-34), and Corinth (18:1-18a), before finally returning to Antioch (18:18b-22). On the journey back he stopped at Ephesus and ministered briefly in the Jewish synagogue; then he proceeded to Caesarea, went to Jerusalem to greet the church, and finally arrived in Antioch of Syria.

The Third Missionary Journey of Paul (18:23–21:1)

Luke recounts this third missionary journey by briefly saying that Paul "went from one place to the next through the region of Galatia and Phrygia, strengthening all the disciples" (18:23). Then he mentions the ministry of

Aquila and Priscilla in the life of Apollos in explaining to him "the way of God more accurately" (18:24-28). Apollos knew only the "baptism of John" and so needed to learn the fundamentals of the faith. He became greatly used of God. We should thank God for people like Aquila and Priscilla who have had a positive influence in our lives so that we have been enabled to serve Him effectively.

The story of Apollos becomes the transition to Paul's ministry in Ephesus (19:1-41). When Paul reached Ephesus (19:1-7) he met some men who, like Apollos, knew only the baptism of John. Paul ministered to them so that they came to know and believe the fullness of the Christian faith. From this experience Paul began to preach to the Jewish people in Ephesus (19:8-9a) but was not too successful. He departed and began to minister daily in the "hall of Tyrannus. This continued for two years, so that all the residents of Asia [the province] heard the word of the Lord, both Jews and Greeks" (19:9-10). All kinds of people were saved in Ephesus including those who had been in the occult and paganism (19:11-20). At this point Luke gives us the fifth of his success-indicators: "So the word of the Lord continued to increase and prevail mightily" (19:20). A riot erupted because

Paul's Third Missionary Journey

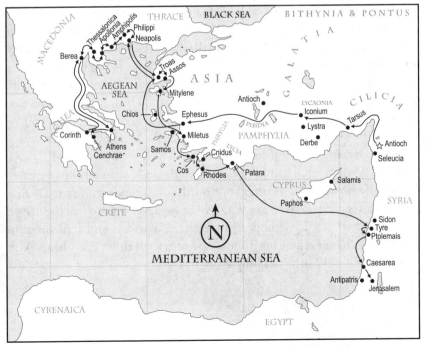

the preaching of the Gospel and the salvation of souls had adversely affected the pagan religious commercialism (sale of silver shrines of Artemis). Paul was protected by God from harm and danger and left Ephesus shortly after the riot had subsided (19:21-41; 20:1).

The third missionary journey concluded with Paul revisiting churches he established in Macedonia and Greece on the second journey (20:1-2a), then heading back through Macedonia to Troas (20:2b-12), then on to Miletus (20:13-38), where he met with the Ephesian elders and encouraged them in the faith. Leaving Miletus he sailed to Syria, landing at Tyre where he found believers and had fellowship with them for seven days (21:1-6). These disciples warned Paul not to go to Jerusalem. Leaving Tyre he sailed to Ptolemais (21:7) where he stayed a day, and then he went on to Caesarea to the house of Philip the evangelist. There Agabus the prophet predicted that Paul would be arrested and imprisoned in Jerusalem (21:8-14). After an unspecified amount of time, Paul and his companions finally arrived in Jerusalem (21:15-17) where they were gladly received by the brethren.

The Arrest and Imprisonment of Paul (21:18–28:31)

Paul was arrested in the temple area (21:18-40) and this prevented his death by his bloodthirsty Jewish brethren. He defended himself before the Jewish multitude (22:1-20), and then specifically before the Jewish high court known as the Sanhedrin (23:1-10). There was a plot to kill him which was unsuccessful (23:11-22), and so the Romans took him to Caesarea for protective custody (23:23-35). Paul was imprisoned in Caesarea for a period of two years and during that time defended himself before Felix (24:1-27), Festus (25:1-27), and King Agrippa II (26:1-32). When he was before Festus (25:10, 12, 25) he appealed to stand before Caesar and be judged. The rest of the book of Acts (27–28) tells the story of Paul's voyage to Rome and his two-year house arrest in which he was allowed to have visitors and carry on a ministry even though chained to a Roman guard. Eventually he was released and continued his apostolic ministry. During his two years of house arrest he wrote what we have come to call the Prison Epistles, which are Ephesians, Philippians, Colossians and Philemon. In these letters he mentions his imprisonment several times and always with a positive outlook, such as Philippians 1:12-26.

The Holy Spirit in the Book of Acts

Luke uses the word *spirit* (*pneuma*) 70 times in the book of Acts. In fifty-seven of these 70 occurrences the word *spirit* refers to the Holy Spirit, three times to the human spirit of man, two times to good angelic spirits, and eight times to demonic spirits. Luke's emphasis in Acts is on the work of the Holy Spirit rather than His person. He does refer to the Spirit as being God (connect Acts 5:3, "lie to the Holy Spirit" with 5:4, "lied to ... God"), but it is

> In the book of Acts, Luke emphasizes what the Spirit does in and through believers.

what the Spirit does in and through believers that is his emphasis. At some point in your study of Scripture you should take the time to go through Acts and make a list of things that the Spirit does–such as baptizes, fills, teaches, guides, etc.

Interpreting the Book of Acts

Conservative evangelical Christians have different approaches to the interpretation of Acts. Some look upon Acts as both *historic* (sharing the events in the story) and *preceptive* (giving teaching or instruction). By this they mean that some of the things in Acts are strictly historical and non-repeatable like casting lots for guidance (Acts 1), speaking in tongues (Acts 2), healing ministry (Acts 3), etc. In other words, these things were done in the early church according to God's will, but are not necessarily to be done today since we have the complete Word of God in the Bible. Those who hold this view believe that Acts is often preceptive. That is, there are things in Acts that should be followed today like baptism, the Lord's Supper, evangelism, Christian love as shown in sharing one's material goods, etc. The rule for determination in this view as to what is merely historic and what is preceptive is what the Epistles say. The Epistles are the doctrinal books of the New Testament and we should make our judgments about Acts from the standpoint of their doctrinal perspectives.

Another interpretive approach to Acts is sometimes labeled *charismatic*. Though there are varying views within this viewpoint, this approach basically says that everything in the book of Acts is experientially duplicative. That is, that everything the early church did may, can, and should be practiced today.

It is the viewpoint of this author that the first interpretive approach is the correct one. However, we should not let differences of interpretive approaches to Acts cause us to be unloving toward our fellow believers in the body of Christ. Acts is a book that ought to challenge us to zeal in preaching the Gospel and in building up one another in the faith.

> **Acts is a book that ought to challenge us to zeal in preaching the Gospel and in building up one another in the faith.**

The book of Acts covers approximately a 30-year period of time. During that period the Gospel was preached from Jerusalem to Rome, souls were saved, churches were established, and many of Paul's letters to the young churches were written. It is these letters, and others that he wrote, plus the General Epistles (Hebrews through Jude) written by James, Peter, John and Jude, which we will now consider in our survey of the New Testament.

LESSON 3 EXAM

Use the exam sheet at the back of the book to complete your exam.

1. In terms of literary style, the Gospel of John is
   A. plain.   C. tedious.
   B. profound.   D. detailed.

2. A negative characteristic of the Apostle John was
   A. a narrow and exclusive spirit.
   B. a revengeful spirit.
   C. a selfish spirit.
   D. all of the above.

3. John 13:l–17:26 is called the
   A. Sermon on the Mount.
   B. Upper Room Discourse.
   C. Sending Out of the Twelve.
   D. Olivet Discourse.

4. John's portrait of Jesus is that of
   A. judge.   C. priest.
   B. prophet.   D. God.

5. The purpose of John's Gospel is stated in
   A. 20:30-31.   C. 5:24-30.
   B. 1:19-28.   D. 12:27-36.

6. Without the book of Acts we would not know about the
   A. choosing of a new Apostle.
   B. arrival of the Holy Spirit.
   C. formation of the church.
   D. all of the above.

7. The geographic pattern of Gospel witness is given in
   A. Acts 5:12-16.   C. Acts 11:19-26.
   B. Acts 8:4-8.   D. Acts 1:8.

8. The plan of the author of Acts was to record the history of the early church up to Paul's ministry in
    A. Damascus.   C. Rome.
    B. Antioch.   D. Spain.

9. Most of Acts 1–12 is devoted to the ministry of
    A. Peter.   C. John.
    B. Stephen.   D. Philip.

10. Paul's missionary travels (Acts 13:1–21:17) consist of
    A. two journeys.   C. four journeys.
    B. three journeys.   D. five journeys.

What Do You Say?

What was John's reason for writing according to John 20:31, and what is your response to this?

_____

_____

_____

_____

Romans and 1 Corinthians

FRIEND

THE LETTER TO THE ROMANS

The Author

According to Romans 1:1, Paul wrote this letter: "Paul, a servant of Christ Jesus, called to be an apostle, set apart for the Gospel of God." In fact, as before mentioned, Paul was the author of 13 letters, and some make it 14 by attributing the anonymous book of Hebrews to him. Romans 16:22 says that Tertius wrote Romans, but that only means that he was Paul's amanuensis (secretary). The content of Romans was Paul's.

The Readers

Paul wrote "To all those in Rome who are loved by God and called to be saints" (Rom. 1:7). As you can see, Paul did not address Romans to a single church. It may be inferred from Romans 16:3-16 that there was more than one church in the city of Rome (16:5, 15). Though Paul had never been in Rome he knew several of the believers in that city as seen from the list of his greetings in chapter 16.

Date and Place of Writing

Paul was in Greece (Achaia)—probably the city of Corinth—when he wrote Romans (compare Acts 20:1-3 with Romans 16:1-2). He was at the end of his third missionary journey which, was about AD 58. He expressed that he had "often intended" to visit the Roman believers (Rom. 1:13), but had been "hindered until now" (Rom. 1:13; 15:22-29). Some think that since Phoebe was going to Rome that Paul asked her to carry the letter to the Roman believers (Rom. 16:1-2). Phoebe was from Cenchrea, which was the port of the city of Corinth.

The Origin of the Roman Church

This is uncertain. Some think that Jewish visitors to Jerusalem from Rome on the day of Pentecost (Acts 2:10) heard the Gospel, believed, and took the good news back to Rome where others heard and were saved. Others think that teachers from the church in Antioch in Syria (a Gentile center for Christianity) evangelized in Rome and many were saved. Still others believe Peter visited the imperial city before AD 50 and started the church. All of these are possibilities, but not being certain which one is correct does not affect our understanding this greatest of Paul's letters. The church must have been long established at the time Paul wrote since he spoke of it as having a worldwide reputation for faith (Rom. 1:8).

The Purpose in Writing Romans

From the content of Romans it seems clear that Paul's chief purpose was to give to Roman believers a clear presentation of the Gospel which he preached and taught wherever he went. Paul was planning to visit the Roman church (Rom. 1:11-15; 15:22-24) and what better way to prepare for his visit than to summarize for them the message which had totally captivated his heart and mind, and transformed his life from an opposer of the Gospel and persecutor of the church to its most passionate promoter.

The General Structure of the Book of Romans

The general structure of Romans is very apparent as one reads through this most systematic of Paul's letters. He begins with an *introduction* (1:1-17) which ends in verses 16 and 17 with a statement of his theme: the Gospel of Christ. He continues with the main body of the letter in which he emphasizes three things: (1) *humanity's problem and God's solution* (1:18–8:3); (2) *Israel's problem and God's solution* (9–11); and finally (3) *service, the outcome of a righteous relationship with God through Christ* (12–15:13). Romans ends with a lengthy *conclusion* (15:14–16:27) in which Paul speaks on a personal level concerning his ministry and future plans. He sends greetings to many.

The Flow of Development of Romans

1. The Introduction (1:1-17)

The introduction consists of a salutation (1:1-7), thanksgiving and prayer (1:8-12), an explanation as to why Paul had not yet visited Rome (1:13-15), and concludes with Paul's theme—the Gospel (1:16-17). All 17 verses are rich in truth and practical application. Let us, however, just briefly touch on the theme—*the Gospel*—of which Paul was "not ashamed." Observe the following breakdown:

1. Nature of the Gospel—"the power of God"
2. Aim of the Gospel—"for salvation"
3. Scope and Condition of the Gospel—"to everyone who believes"
4. Historic Pattern of the Gospel—"to the Jew first and also for the Greeks"
5. Revelation in the Gospel—"the righteousness of God"
6. Principle of the Gospel—"from faith for faith"
7. Confirmation of the Gospel—"as it is written, The righteous shall live by faith"

It is no wonder Paul is proud of the Gospel! It does for people what they cannot do for themselves through law, ritual, and works. One simply believes and salvation is immediately received! This blessed theme will be expanded and explained by Paul in 3:21–5:21.

2. Humanity's Problem (1:18-3:20)

Paul makes it very clear in this section why everyone—Gentile and Jewish—needs the Gospel. It is because all people are under the wrath of God because of sin. It is not merely that all human beings are sinners. Humanity is in constant jeopardy of the wrath of God because of sin. This section breaks down into three parts.

1. The Gentile world is under God's wrath because of sin (1:18-32)
2. The Jewish world is under God's wrath because of sin (2:1–3:8)
3. Paul concludes that all (Jewish people and Gentiles) are under wrath because of sin (3:9-20)

3. God's Solution for Humanity (3:21–8:39)

There is only one way out of the problem—God! He removes the wrath which is due to sin and provides righteousness (3:21–5:21) and sanctification (6:1–8:39). Righteousness is a right legal standing before God, the judge. Sanctification refers to our new position before God as holy with a new ability to live holy lives.

Righteousness—The Believer's New Legal Standing Before God (3:21–5:21)

Paul develops this truth in three parts. First he speaks of the *provision of legal righteousness* (3:21-31). He makes it clear that this righteousness for the believer is apart from the Law of Moses, that it is based on the work of Christ (redemption, propitiation), that it is received by faith alone, and that it establishes (conforms to, confirms) the Old Testament Scriptures (3:31).

Secondly, Paul speaks of the *proof of legal righteousness* by faith (4:1-25). What proof is there of Paul's teaching that faith-righteousness does indeed conform to the Old Testament (3:31) and is therefore not contradictory to what Old Testament believers taught? Proof is abundant and

> **Righteousness for the believer is based on the work of Christ, and it is received by faith alone.**

Paul uses Abraham, the originator of the Jewish race, as his prime example. All Jewish people would agree that Abraham was righteous before God. But how did he get his righteousness? Paul clearly and ably demonstrates that it was not by works (4:1-8), not by ritual circumcision (4:9-12), and not by the law (4:13-17). Rather, it was simply by faith (4:3, 18-25).

Thirdly, Paul speaks of the *permanence of righteousness* by faith (5:1-21). Just how permanent is a righteousness for which a person doesn't work, but instead simply receives by faith? Can it be lost? The answer is a resounding no! Paul argues from three points of view to demonstrate its permanence. First there is the argument from experience (5:1-5). Will the trials of life destroy our righteous standing before God which was received by justification by faith? No! The trials of life strengthen our faith and promote character (5:3-5). Secondly, there is the argument from the logic of God's love (5:6-11). That is, if God loved us (past) "while we were still sinners," *how much more,* now that we are saints (present) will He preserve us (future) from the wrath to come. Paul's third argument is from the representative headship of Jesus Christ in comparison with Adam. Just as the one act of Adam in the garden of Eden brought sin and death to the race, so the one act of Jesus Christ upon the cross brought righteousness and life (5:12, 21). Paul makes it clear that these gifts are not automatic, they must be received (5:17).

Sanctification—The Believer's Position of Holiness Before God (6:1–8:39)

Humanity is not only guilty before God and so under God's wrath, but also under the power and authority of sin—a slave to sin.

This is where Romans 6–8 comes in. Here Paul demonstrates that the believer is no longer under sin's power and authority, and therefore is no longer obligated to sin. Thus, living a life of holiness on earth—which is God's will for all—is made possible. Paul makes it abundantly clear that sanctification (holiness) is the believer's new standing (position) in Christ and is to be the believer's condition (state) on a day-to-day basis. Let us observe how this major section develops:

1. The believer has been liberated from sin (6:1-23) by becoming united to Christ (6:1-14), and enslaved to God (6:15-23).
2. The believer has been liberated from the Law of Moses (7:1-6). This does not infer that the Law is sinful. It is holy, just, and good (7:7-13). However, the good law cannot produce a holy life in the believer, which was Paul's own testimony (7:14-25).
3. The believer has been liberated and empowered through the Holy Spirit (8:1-39) to live a life pleasing to God.
4. Our liberation makes practical holiness a daily possibility (6:11-14, 19-22; 7:6; 8:12-17).

Humanity has a problem. All people are under wrath because of sin. God's solution is justification and sanctification based on the work of Christ on the cross and realized through the work of the Holy Spirit. Let me ask you, are you one of God's justified ones? If not, why not today? Receive Jesus by faith (4:4-8).

4. Israel's Problem (9:1-10:21)

It would be natural for Paul to leave chapter eight and move on to the practical teaching of 12:1–15:13. Before he does that he must deal with a problem which he must have confronted whenever he preached to a Jewish audience. What about the Jewish nation? Is God finished with Israel because of their unbelief? Did not God promise unconditionally in the Hebrew Scriptures a Jewish Kingdom with Messiah ruling over it? Yes!

Then how do we reconcile the fact that Israel rejected Messiah, and that God has established a new community called the Church? Does this not mean that God's unconditional promises to the Jewish people have been aborted? This may not have meant a lot to Gentile Christians in Paul's day (and even Gentile believers today!) but it was a very serious issue that had to be answered so as not to hinder the preaching of the Gospel to Jewish people. Paul's thought develops as follows:

Israel Has Been Rejected by God Because They Have Rejected the Messiah

Paul begins with strong emotion. He has great sorrow and grief in his heart for his unbelieving Jewish brethren—especially in the light of the great position and privileges of the nation (9:1-6). However, in a lengthy section (9:6-29) he makes no excuses for Israel. Rather he defends the justice of God's rejection of the nation.

Actually, God's rejection of the nation was predicted in the Old Testament (see 9:25-29) so this should not be a surprise.

Paul explains in detail (9:30–10:21) that God's rejection of the Jewish nation was due to Israel's rejection of Messiah. The Jewish nation sought righteousness by the Law and the Gentiles by faith (9:30-33). The Jewish people were blind to Gospel righteousness (10:1-15). Gospel righteousness teaches that Christ is the end of the Law for righteousness (10:1-4). It teaches that righteousness is free to all. One does not have to work for it (10:5-10). It teaches that righteousness is offered to all—both Jewish peoples and Gentiles (10:11-15). Once again, this rejection was predicted in their own Scriptures (10:16-21). What is the answer to this problem of rejection in the light of the unconditional promises of God? Paul gives a clear and satisfying answer in chapter 11.

> **Doctrine should transform the way we think, our attitudes, our goals and ambitions, and our conduct toward God and man.**

5. God's Solution for Israel (11:1-36)

The Restoration of Israel

This solution falls into two lines of argument. First, Paul argues, the rejection of Israel is not total (11:1-10). Paul teaches that God always has His remnant (11:5-7)—even now—and he illustrates this from the life of Elijah (11:1-4). The second line of argument is that God's rejection of

Israel is not final (11:11-36). The nation has been temporarily set aside in the purposes of God and it is experiencing a judicial "hardening" (11:25). This hardening will go on until "the fullness of the Gentiles has come in" (11:25). The fullness of the Gentiles is the present church age which will come to an end when Jesus raptures the church to heaven (1 Thess. 4:14-18). In the meantime, Israel's rejection means blessing for the whole world (11:11-12, 28-32). Paul is overwhelmed by the glory of God's great plan of salvation and utters one of the great doxologies of the Bible (11:33-36).

6. Service, the Outcome of a Right Relationship to God (12:1–15:13)

Doctrine should transform the way we think, our attitudes, our goals and ambitions, and our conduct toward God and man. True to his pattern, Paul, as he does in his other letters, exhorts us to live out the doctrine as we attempt to serve our Lord. Paul speaks of our service in relation to several areas:

- Service in relation to God—consecration (12:1-2)
- Service in relation to the church—humility (12:3-8)
- Service in relation to all men—love (12:9-21)
- Service in relation to the state—subjection (13:1-7)
- Service in relation to society—be a good neighbor (13:8-14)
- Service in relation to the weak and strong brethren (14:1-13)
- Consideration of one another in matters of Christian liberty (14:14–15:13)

7. Conclusion to the Book of Romans (15:14–16:27)

Paul concludes Romans with a personal narrative (15:14-33), the commendation of Phoebe (16:1-2), greetings to many members of the Roman church (16:3-16), a warning to Roman believers (16:17-20), greetings to the Romans from some brethren who were with Paul as he wrote (16:21-24), and a final doxology (16:25-27). This conclusion, like the introduction, is full of rich truth and practical application which should not be neglected in any serious study of Romans.

THE FIRST LETTER TO THE CORINTHIANS

Background on the City of Corinth

In 1954, I, along with several others, visited the ancient ruins of the city of Corinth. It was very interesting to see the city where, centuries before, the Apostle Paul had ministered the Gospel seeing many saved and a church established (Acts 18). Corinth was located near the southern end of the isthmus which connected the continent with Achaia. In the Roman world, the city of Corinth was designated a Roman colony. In a sense, a Roman colony was a little bit of Rome away from Rome. Thus, those living in Corinth had all the rights and privileges of those living in Rome. Corinth was the capital of Achaia and the Roman Pro-Consul Gallio was in office when Paul made his first visit to that city (Acts 18).

Hundreds of thousands lived in Corinth at the time of Paul. The inhabitants were a mixture of Romans, Greeks and Jewish. It was, because of its population size and location, an ideal place to preach the Gospel and establish a church.

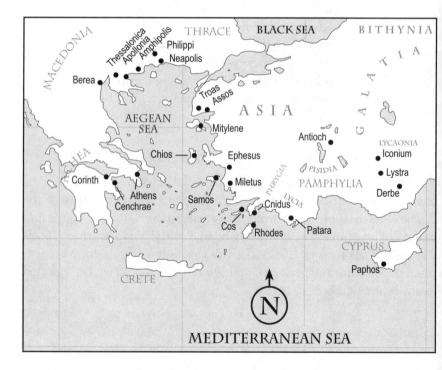

In terms of culture, Corinth never became famous for philosophy like Athens. However it was famous for arts and architecture.

Paganism was strong in Corinth and immorality was a part of its paganistic worship. In fact, on the Acro-Corinthus was a heathen temple dedicated to Aphrodite, the goddess of love. Hundreds of prostitutes were involved in its ritual. Thus, it is not difficult to discern how the very name of the city, Corinth, became synonymous with immorality. Corinth was a city in desperate need of the Gospel and God so arranged that Paul should spend 18 months preaching that liberating good news.

The Author

According to the salutation (1:1), Paul wrote 1 Corinthians. He included with him in the salutation the name of a fellow believer ("our brother"), Sosthenes. It is not known for certain if this man is to be identified with the one by the same name in Acts 18:17. If it is the same person then he must have been converted later and became a traveling companion with Paul.

The Readers

Paul speaks of his believing Corinthian readers as "sanctified in Christ Jesus, called to be saints" (1:2). These descriptions ("sanctified … called to be saints") are all the more significant given the fact that the Corinthian church was very carnal (compare 1 Cor. 3:1-9)! The readership is not limited just to the Corinthian church. Paul broadens it to "all those who in every place call upon the name of our Lord Jesus Christ, both their Lord and ours." This reminds us that though a book of Scripture may have been sent to a particular church to help them with their peculiar problems, that all believers may benefit from its truth.

The Origin of the Corinthian Church

Paul preached the Gospel in Corinth toward the end of his second missionary journey (Acts 18). He went to Corinth after his ministry in Athens (Acts 17:16-34). In Corinth, he found two Jewish people, a husband and wife named Aquila and Priscilla, with whom he stayed and worked (Paul and Aquila were both tent-makers). Every Sabbath he would preach in the synagogue, but when Silas and Timothy joined him from Macedonia he devoted full time to the ministry. Though there was persecution, God encouraged Paul in preaching so that over an 18 month period many were saved and the church was established (Acts 18:1-11). This church turned out to be one of the most spiritually enriched and gifted churches Paul ever founded (1 Cor. 1:4-8). However, spiritual wealth and gifts for ministry do not ensure spirituality!

The Date, Place and Occasion of Writing 1 Corinthians

Chronologically, 1 Corinthians comes before Romans. Recall that Paul wrote Romans around AD 58 toward the end of the third missionary journey. He wrote 1 Corinthians on the third missionary journey around AD 54 or 55 when he was ministering in the city of Ephesus. We know he wrote from Ephesus, as can be gathered from 1 Corinthians 16:8 where he says, "But I will tarry in Ephesus until Pentecost." Compare this with 16:19 where Paul mentions the churches of Asia (Ephesus was in that province) and sends greetings from Aquila and Priscilla and the church meeting in their house.

The occasion for writing is given in 1 Corinthians 1:10-17. Paul had received information from the household of Chloe that the church was having disruptive problems (1–6) among the believers which, if not ministered to, would threaten the very existence of the church. Also, the Corinthians had perplexing questions of a doctrinal and practical nature which needed to be answered.

The Purpose in Writing 1 Corinthians

The purpose comes out of the occasion. Paul sat down with pen in hand for the purpose of rectifying the immoral situation described in chapters 1–6, and to give understanding regarding the puzzling questions asked in correspondence to him (17:1–16:24). If the Corinthians would give heed to his wisdom and exhortations, then harmony and love among the members would be restored.

The Theme of 1 Corinthians

The theme is practical sanctification. The Corinthians had experienced positional sanctification when they were saved. Now they must build on that by living holy lives. Giving sincere and heartfelt heed to Paul's instruction would go a long way in producing Christ-likeness in them.

We all need to ask the question from time to time: "If every church member were just like me, what kind of a church would my church be?"

We do not get over all our problems and sins when we are first saved. We are forgiven all immediately upon salvation, but practical sanctification takes a lifetime to accomplish. We should be sensitive to the need of freeing ourselves from negative patterns and habits which bring grief and disunity to God's people. The Corinthians evidently brought a lot of "baggage" with them from their old lives into the fellowship at Corinth. They needed to change and so do we.

> **We should be sensitive to the need of freeing ourselves from negative patterns and habits which bring grief and disunity to God's people.**

Some Points of Interest

There are many of these in this important letter, but the following are emphasized: First, there is an emphasis on local church problems and how to solve them. Thus, 1 Corinthians becomes a valuable book from which to obtain wisdom in problem-solving. Another point of interest is the emphasis on spiritual gifts. The most complete instruction on this subject in the New Testament is 1 Corinthians 12–14. Finally, the most detailed and complete instruction in the New Testament on the doctrine of resurrection is found in chapter 15.

General Structure of 1 Corinthians

1. Introduction (1:1-9)
2. Correction of Disruptive Problems in the Church (1:10–6:20)
3. Counsel Concerning Perplexing Problems in the Church (7:1–15:58)
4. Conclusion (16:1-24)

The Flow of Development of 1 Corinthians

1. Introduction (1:1-9)

Paul begins with a salutation (1:1-3) in which he identifies himself as "an apostle of Jesus Christ." Thus what he has to say to the Corinthians and others who will read the letter is authoritative and to be heeded. After wishing them "grace ... and peace" he moves on to offer thanksgiving to God (1:4-9) for the grace shown to the Corinthians and what that entails. From this brief introduction, Paul proceeds to minister to the moral problems at Corinth.

2. Correction of Disruptive Problems in the Church (1:1–6:20)

Satan hates the church and will try in any way, and at any cost, to destroy its unity and ministry. Chapters one through six, to the sensitive Christian, is a heartbreaking record of the power and influence of the flesh. Paul deals with the following sins of the church:

The Disruptive Sin of Divisions (1:10–4:21)

In their carnality, believers in Corinth had created four factions centered around four personalities: Paul, Apollos, Peter, and Christ (1:12). This is so unreasonable since, among others things, Christ is not divided (1:13-17). Paul seeks to remedy the situation by getting the believers to refocus on the two things that will bind them together in love and humility. What are these? First, the preaching of the cross (1:18–3:4). Paul did not preach human philosophy to the believers in Corinth. He preached "Jesus Christ and Him crucified" (2:2). They need to turn their eyes back on the person and work of Christ and away from humans and human philosophy. The second thing is to properly evaluate Christian workers– whoever they are (3:5–4:21). Workers, Paul says, are to be looked upon only as servants (3:5-9). They are not gods. They are not to be exalted above one another. They are to work together to accomplish God's will. God will give the blessing now and rewards later on for faithful service (3:10-17; 4:1-5). Knowing and applying the truth of this section is basic to maturing into a fruitful servant of Christ.

The Disruptive Sin of Sexual Immorality (5:1-13)

A man in the church had committed incest with his father's wife and some in the church were actually glorying in it (5:1-2). Paul called for removal of the offender and then rebuked the church for allowing this "leaven" (a symbol of sinful behavior) to corrupt the church (5:3-8). Paul had written a previous letter to Corinth in which he had instructed the believers to not keep company with immoral people. They misunderstood him to mean unbelievers. He actually meant immoral believers. So he clarified his meaning and once again commanded to put the sinning brother out of fellowship (5:9-13).

The Disruptive Sin of Lawsuits Against Believers (6:1-11)

Believers are forbidden to take fellow believers to law. To do so, Paul says, is to deny our future calling (6:1-3) of judging along with Christ. It defies logic (6:4-6) for the unbelieving judge is unfit to judge in matters of the church. It is a defrauding of our brother (6:7-8)—a form of revenge—which shows no love. Finally, it disregards our deliverance (6:9-11). We were saved from an evil background. To pursue lawsuits is to live like we used to when unconverted. This teaching is very much needed in our modern world because it is being violated by believers.

The Disruptive Sin of Abusing Christian Liberty (6:12-20)

Christian liberty was not well understood by the Corinthians. It is a subject that Paul will say more about in chapters 8–10. When Paul says in 6:12 that "All things are lawful for me, but all things are not helpful," he is referring to non-moral things such as food, drink, etc. Obviously there are things that are not lawful for a believer to do, things that are in the area of morals and ethics. The Corinthians' understanding was simple: Hunger is a legitimate desire and one may satisfy it at any time (6:13). Sex is a legitimate, God-given desire and one may satisfy it at anytime. It sounds logical, doesn't it? But sex is not in the category of non-moral things. The believer, Paul says, is not to use their body for sexual immorality (6:13b-18). The believer's body is the temple of the Holy Spirit and it has been purchased with the precious blood of Christ. Therefore the believing Christian is to glorify God in their body (6:19-20). Modern thinking disagrees with this. Today's philosophy is, "If it feels good, do it!" God has commanded us to live by His law, not by our feelings!

The believing Christian is to glorify God in his body.

3. Counsel Concerning Perplexing Problems (7:1–15:58)

As we have seen, some from the household of Chloe had informed Paul of some terribly disruptive problems in the church at Corinth. Paul ministered to these problems in chapters 1–6. Chapter seven begins with, "Now concerning the things of which you wrote to me …." This expression, used several times more in the following chapters, refers to a letter written by the Corinthians asking for wisdom on how to deal with problems in the church which were not of a moral nature. There are six of these problems—problems which every generation of the church for the past 2,000 years has faced. Paul's solutions to the problems are still up-to-date and very practical. Let us briefly note the areas of difficulty:

Concerning Marriage (7:1-40)

In this chapter, Paul gives counsel to both the unmarried and the married. The chapter breaks down as follows: (1) Paul teaches that marriage is advisable (7:1-7) because it is the norm. Celibacy is the exception. (2) Paul, having put forth the general principle, now deals with specific categories (7:8-40). These are the unmarried and the widow (7:8-9), the married person (7:10-11), the believer married to an unbeliever (7:12-24), virgin women (7:25-38), and widows (7:39-40).

Concerning Christian Liberty (8:10–10:33)

Paul touched on this subject in 6:12-20. The stimulus for this instruction was the problem that early Christians had concerning the eating of meat offered in sacrifice to idols. This was an acute problem as seen by the fact that three chapters are devoted to it here, and that Paul also had to deal with it in Romans 14:1–15:13. The person who is fully liberated in regard to non-moral things says, "I know ..." and "I have a right ..." The person who was *not* fully liberated in regard to non-moral things, whom Paul calls the weaker brother (that is, weak in understanding), felt that eating meat that had been previously offered in sacrifice to a pagan idol was really idolatrous. There is really nothing moral or immoral about a piece of meat no matter what it has been through. The "weak," however, had a conscience about it.

> The goal of each believer should be to love their brothers and sisters in Christ.

How does Paul deal with this delicate and tension-filled issue? First, he instructs the fully liberated brother that "knowledge" is not enough. Knowledge makes one proud. There needs to be self-denying, self-disciplining love so that the weaker brother does not stumble and become a spiritual casualty (1 Cor. 8). Secondly, Paul goes on to enforce his instruction on the need for self-denying love and discipline. He does this by positive (9:1-27) and negative (10:1-13) illustrations. He used his life and ministry as a positive example of the exercise of discipline in the realm of Christian liberty. This is followed by the negative example of Israel. Thirdly, the apostle applies his guidance to the present situation of the Corinthian church (10:14-30). They should not participate in heathen feasts (10:14-22); they should eat meat bought in the market without investigating where it came from (10:23-26); they should eat meat in a private home setting without investigating where it came from (10:27-30); and finally Paul gives a good principle to follow for any situation in life: "So, whether you eat or drink, or whatever you do, do all to the glory of God" (10:31-33).

The goal of each believer should be to love their brothers and sisters in Christ (John 13:34-35). Is this too much to ask in the light of the fact that Christ loved us even to death? Denying ourselves for the sake of others is Christian!

Concerning Public Worship (11:1-34)

This chapter coverings two topics that were involved when the church gathered to worship. The first topic is the use and significance of head coverings for women during the church gathering. Men are instructed not to cover their heads.

The second deals with the Lord's Supper or communion (11:17-34). The conduct of believers at the Lord's Supper was spiritually unhealthy (11:17-22). Paul sought to rectify the situation by reminding them of the institution of the supper by Jesus (11:23), and its memorial character. The bread is a symbol of His body and the cup a symbol of His blood (11:24-26). He called for self-examination before partaking of the elements (11:27-28), and he warned of judgment upon any who would eat and drink in an unworthy manner (11:29). Actually, God had afflicted some with sickness and removed others through death because of unconfessed and unjudged sin (11:30-34).

The Lord's Supper is the central worship meeting of the church. It is a time when believers may focus their entire attention upon their Lord and Savior and praise Him for who He is and what He has accomplished at the cross. The preaching of the word may stimulate worship (praise and thanksgiving to God), but the Lord's Supper is the worship meeting of the church that is focused completely on Christ. In the early church, believers remembered the Lord in the communion each Sunday ("On the first day of the week, when we were gathered together to break bread" in Acts 20:7).

Concerning Spiritual Gifts (12:1–14:40)

Paul said in chapter one that the Corinthian church was a greatly gifted church: "You were enriched in Him in all speech and all knowledge … you are not lacking in any gift …" (1:5, 7). A "gift" is a supernatural ability with which to serve the Lord. The subject of gifts must have been of primary interest to the Corinthians for Paul gives three chapters of explanation.

It is easy to follow this section as seen by the following outline:

1. *The Validity of Gifts (12:1-3).* How can one determine if a gifted person is true or false? By the content of the message. Does he or she curse or acknowledge the Lordship of Christ?

2. *The Unity of Gifts (12:4-6).* In paganism, certain manifestations might be attributed to different demonic spirits. Spiritual gifts, however, in their variety, use and results, are all from ONE God.

3. *The Purpose of Gifts (12:7).* The purpose of gifts is for the mutual profit of each person in the church. Your gift is not for your benefit but for the common good of others. Any blessing we receive in the use of our gifts is just the by-product of using the gift, not the purpose.

4. *The Listing of the Gifts (12:8-10).* There is a total of nine gifts in these verses. Some of them are repeated in 12:28-31 while three new ones (apostles, helps, administrations) are added. Thus, a total of 12 different gifts is listed. There are other gift passages (Rom. 12, Eph. 4, 1 Peter 4). In all, Paul lists 19 different spiritual gifts.

5. *The Principles Governing the Use of Gifts (12:11–14:26).* First, there is the principle of sovereignty (12:11, 18) which means that God gives the believer his/her gift/gifts and places him/her in the body where it pleases Him. Then there is the principle of love. Paul devotes a whole chapter to this (13:1-13). Actually, this principle is found in all the gift passages. Finally there is the principle of edification (14:1-26), which deals with the building up of the body of Christ. If we live by these principles, it will keep us from becoming jealous, discouraged, cruel, and selfish.

6. *The Restrictions Governing the Use of Some Gifts (14:27-40).* Paul placed restrictions on the use of the gifts of prophecy and tongues. These gifts were being abused. Everything, Paul says, is to be "done decently and in order" (14:40).

Concerning the Resurrection (15:1-58)

This is one of the most important chapters in the Bible. It is a companion to all the resurrection accounts in the Gospels. The Gospel, which basically is the death, burial, and resurrection of Jesus (15:1-4), is not something Paul invented. It was predicted in the Old Testament. There were many witnesses to the bodily resurrection of Jesus (15:5-11). Yet this evidence was not being believed. What was the problem? Some were still holding to the Greek philosophical view of Plato of no bodily resurrection (15:12-19). If there is no such a thing as bodily resurrection from the dead, then that would mean that Jesus is not risen—with the further implication, among other things, that we are still in our sins. But Christ has indeed risen (15:20-34) as the first of a brand new order of people who will rise to die no more. Because He lives, our mortal souls will put on immortality and our corruptible bodies will put on incorruption (15:34-57).

In view of our hope, Paul says, we should never give up but keep on standing fast and serving because our labor is not in vain in the Lord (15:58).

4. The Conclusion (16:1-24)

Paul closes the letter by exhorting the believers to be preparing for the collection for the poor believers in Jerusalem (16:1-4). He gives information about his plans for the future—including a visit to Corinth (16:5-12). He exhorted them to diligence in faith and to let love characterize all they do (16:13-14). He commended certain ones who wonderfully manifested Christ in their lives (16:15-18), and finished with greetings (16:19-21), a warning (16:22), and a benediction (16:23-24).

This is one of the most practical letters in the New Testament and deserves to be diligently studied and applied.

LESSON 4 EXAM

Use the exam sheet at the back of the book to complete your exam.

1. **The chief purpose of Romans was to**
   A. deal with church problems.
   B. encourage believers to avoid idolatry.
   C. give a clear presentation of the Gospel Paul taught.
   D. encourage evangelism.

2. **In Romans 1:18–3:20, Paul emphasized**
   A. man's problem and God's solution.
   B. Israel's problems and God's solution.
   C. service in Christian living.
   D. all of the above.

3. **The problem in 1:18–3:20 was that all men**
   A. are evil because sin causes insanity.
   B. are under wrath because of sin.
   C. are weakened morally because of sin.
   D. love sin and hate righteousness.

4. **The point of 4:1-25 is that righteousness by faith conforms**
   A. to the Old Testament.
   B. to only a few Biblical writers.
   C. to all religious teaching.
   D. to typical eastern teaching.

5. **Gospel righteousness teaches that**
   A. Christ is the end of the law for righteousness.
   B. righteousness is free to all.
   C. righteousness is offered to all.
   D. all of the above.

6. **Paul preached the Gospel in Corinth over a period of**
   A. one year.   C. two years.
   B. eighteen months.   D. three years.

7. **Paul wrote 1 Corinthians while in the city of**
   A. Troas.   C. Thessalonica.
   B. Sardis.   D. Ephesus.

8. **The theme of 1 Corinthians is**
   A. practical sanctification.
   B. the second coming of Christ.
   C. Christian joy and virtue.
   D. the power of positive thinking.

9. **The first six chapters of 1 Corinthians deal with**
   A. disruptive problems in the church.
   B. dangerous heresy in the church.
   C. doctrinal differences in the church.
   D. none of the above.

10. **One of the perplexing problems which Paul had to deal with in chapters 7–15 was**
    A. sexual immorality.   C. divisions.
    B. marriage.   D. the humanity of Christ.

What Do You Say?

Why is the fact of Christ's resurrection so important? Is it important to you?

_____

_____

_____

_____

LESSON 5

2 Corinthians and Galatians

THE SECOND LETTER TO THE CORINTHIANS

The Author

The Apostle Paul wrote this second letter and he included Timothy with him in the salutation (1:1). Timothy was a young man whom Paul discipled and took along with him on his journeys (Acts 16:1-5). He had great respect and commendation for this young man as illustrated in Philippians 2:19-23. Paul loved to help establish young men in the faith. We should take the time to do the same.

The Readers

Specifically, this letter was sent to the Corinthians and secondarily it was for "all the saints who are in all Achaia." Remember that Achaia was the Greek province in which Corinth was located.

The Date, Place, and Occasion for Writing

Paul had been ministering in Ephesus for at least three years (remember that he wrote 1 Corinthians from there). After sending Timothy and Erastus to Macedonia, persecution broke out against him (Acts 19:21-41). When the uproar had ceased, Paul left for Macedonia. He had hoped to meet Titus along the way in Troas before passing over to Macedonia (compare Acts 20:7-12 with 2 Cor. 2:12-13) but Titus did not show up. Thus, Paul, having no rest in his spirit because of his concern for the Corinthians, went (2 Cor. 7:5-7, 13-16) and heard the good news that his ministry by letter to the Corinthians had been effective. On this occasion he wrote 2 Corinthians and sent it with Titus (compare 2 Cor. 8:16–9:5). This second inspired letter to the Corinthians was written just a few months after 1 Corinthians— possibly in the same year—AD 54 or 55. Paul followed Titus later to Corinth (compare Acts 20:2-3) where he was for three months. Recall that it was during this period that he wrote Romans.

The Theme of 2 Corinthians

The theme of 2 Corinthians is the ministry of the Apostle Paul. The word "ministry" and its various forms are found close to twenty times in the letter; it is a key word. Anyone who wants to be a servant of the Lord should read carefully this very practical letter for principles and illustrations from Paul's life which may be legitimately applied to one's own service.

Some Points of Interest

- It is a very personal letter. We see more the open heart of Paul for the Corinthians than his mind.
- It is a very emotional letter. Paul's concern for the Corinthians causes the extremes of joy and sorrow, of commendation and condemnation. As he wrote, it would seem that his pen was dipped in tears (compare 2 Cor. 7). The reason for much of the negative emotion is the fact that Paul had enemies at Corinth who sought to discredit his life and ministry. They accused him of fickleness (1:17-18, 23), of arrogance (3:1; 5:12), of unclearness in his public preaching (4:3), of being a coward (10:10), of unpleasing personal appearance (4:7-10), of being close to insane (5:13), of not being a genuine apostle (11:5). These attacks cannot go unchallenged! Paul responded firmly, yet with true Christian love. He never despaired of God's erring people. If he did not love them, he would not have bothered with them. He had their best interests at heart.
- It is a very informational letter. For instance, Paul says much about himself not found elsewhere (11:23-28; 11:32; 12:1-4; 12:7-9; etc.).
- There are several mentions of Titus. Titus is never once mentioned in Acts but he is referred to 13 times in Paul's epistles. Nine of these are in 2 Corinthians.

The General Structure of 2 Corinthians

1. The Description of Paul's Apostolic Ministry (1:1–7:16)
2. The Duty of Paul's Apostolic Ministry (8:1–9:15)
3. The Defense of Paul's Apostolic Ministry (10:1–13:14)

The Flow of Development of 2 Corinthians

With the general structure above in mind, let's look at how the text develops in the three sections.

1. The Description of Paul's Apostolic Ministry (1:1–7:16)

Introduction (1:1–2:11)

Paul begins with a lengthy introduction (1:1–2:11) which consists of three points. First he gives his usual salutation (1:1-2), in which he makes the point that his apostleship (questioned by some Corinthians) was by the will of God. He follows this with thanksgiving to God (1:3-11) for His comfort

> **Paul lauds the new covenant because of its greater glory than the old.**

and deliverance. Finally, he explains that he has been a sincere servant of Christ. His sincerity had been questioned by some at Corinth (1:12–2:11). Diligent study of this long introduction will yield to the student many practical principles and lessons for life.

Description of Paul's Ministry (2:12–7:16)

Paul gives a very wonderful description of his ministry, which has been instructive for believers for 2,000 years. There are eight descriptions followed by an appeal. Let us briefly note them:

1. *A Ministry of Triumph (2:12-17).* Paul said that wherever he went God gave him victory in the preaching of the Gospel.
2. *A Ministry of Accreditation (3:1-3).* Paul's credentials were the Corinthians themselves! He didn't need special letters of commendation. The very existence of the church is proof of the validity of Paul's ministry.
3. *A New Covenant Ministry (3:4-18).* Paul praises the new covenant because of its greater glory than the old (4-11), its power to liberate (12-17), and the fact of the possibility of personal transformation

by the Holy Spirit (18). This particular point is aimed at the Judaizers–those who wanted to keep Christians under the legal system of Moses.

4. *A Ministry of Honesty (4:1-6).* Some in Paul's day were self-centered and deceitful in their ministry (like the cults). Paul did not handle the Word of God in this way.

5. *A Ministry of Hope (4:7–5:10).* Believers at that time were in much affliction and suffering. Paul suffered greatly, too. In this section, he gives three aspects of our hope which should serve as incentives to persist in our service for Christ. First, there is the hope of resurrection (4:7-18). Next we have the hope of being in heaven (5:1-9). Finally there is the hope of reward given out at the judgment seat of Christ (5:10).

6. *A Ministry of Transparency (5:11-17).* Some had criticized Paul's behavior as insane. All of Paul's conduct, however, could be explained in one of two ways: either zeal for God (5:13a), or to benefit fellow believers (5:13b). He was motivated on the one hand by the fear of God (5:11), and on the other by the love of Christ (5:14-17).

7. *A Ministry of Reconciliation (5:18–6:2).* Paul considered himself an ambassador for Christ. He called upon all to be reconciled to God through the work of Christ (5:21). We should be proclaiming this message as well!

8. *A Ministry That Had Been Tested and Approved (6:3-10).* Paul's experience in ministry was proof of the sincerity of it. What is the rationale? Simply this: Why should a person go through so much pain and sorrow if their motives were evil?

> **Paul called upon all to be reconciled to God through the work of Christ. We should be proclaiming this message as well!**

9. *Conclusion (6:11–7:16).* Paul closes this description of his ministry by making an appeal to the Corinthians for affection (6:11-13), for separation (6:14–7:1), for reception (7:2-4). He is assured in his own mind that the majority have had a change of heart toward him (7:5-10), and that a new spirit is among them (7:11-12). Their positive reception of Titus gave him confidence of their change (7:13-16).

2. The Duty of Paul's Apostolic Ministry (8:1–9:15)

This duty was the collecting of material goods for the poor saints in Jerusalem. Paul mentions the collection in three passages. He first mentioned it in 1 Corinthians 16:1-4 where he exhorted the Corinthians to start putting aside for it. The second mention is 2 Corinthians 8–9 where he makes his most ardent appeal. The third mention is Romans 15:25-28 where he attests to finally receiving the collection and is ready to take it to Jerusalem.

The Incentives for the Completion of the Collection (8:1-11)

What does it take to get people to give? Money is one of the last things we seem to surrender to the Lord. Paul gives three incentives to motivate the Corinthians:

1. *The Example of the Macedonians (8:1-8).* They were impoverished!
2. *The Example of Jesus Christ (8:9).* He was rich but became poor!
3. *The Example of the Corinthians (8:10-11).* They were the first to promise to give. Now keep the promise!

The Principles for the Completion of the Collection (8:12-24)

They are to give willingly (8:12a), according to ability (8:12b), to create an equality (8:13-15), and put the collection into the hands of tested and approved men for delivery (8:16-24).

The Provocation for the Completion of the Collection (9:1-6)

Paul sought to provoke them to faithfulness to their promise by telling them that he had been boasting to others about the Corinthians' readiness (1–3) and the potential embarrassment to him and them if they are not ready!

The Exhortation for the Completion of the Collection (9:7-11)

Paul exhorts them to do just as they had purposed, not grudgingly or under compulsion, but with a cheerful heart. God loves this kind of giver, and He promises to give them more so that they can give more (9:8)!

The Results of Completing the Collection (9:12-15)

What will be the blessed results of completing this project-giving? First, the needs of others will be met (9:12) with much thanks to God. Secondly, it will be proof to the Jewish people of Gentile salvation (9:13). Thirdly, the Jewish people will reciprocate with prayer-support for the Gentile believers, and in the process their hearts will yearn for them in Christian love (9:14). Paul is overwhelmed by the thought of it all and cries out, "Thanks be to God for His inexpressible gift!" (9:15).

3. The Defense of Paul's Apostolic Ministry (10:1-13:14)

There was probably no more sincere and transparent person in the New Testament among God's servants than Paul. Yet this man suffered greatly at the hands of so-called Christians as well as from Jewish people and pagans. The verbal abuse Paul was receiving at Corinth was geared to bring him down, to discredit him in the eyes of the Corinthians. He must be vindicated, and in these chapters he sets about to do that very thing.

Accusations Brought Against Him (10:1-18)

As Paul reviews the charges brought against him he does so with a great deal of irony. His enemies say that he walks and wars after the flesh (1-6), that he serves without apostolic authority (7-8), that he is cowardly (9-12), that he had no right to minister at Corinth (13-18). These charges he will answer in 11:1–12:13.

Answers to the Accusations (11:1–12:13)

First he deals with his motivation for answering (11:1-4). It is twofold: He has a godly jealously for them (love). After all, he led them to Christ. Then he has fear that Satan, just as he deceived Eve, is deceiving them from their devotion to Christ. Do we have the same kind of jealousy and love for our brethren? Do we watch out for them as Paul did his converts? Many believers have strayed because no shepherd watched over them. Are you presently attempting to shepherd someone?

From his motivation in answering the accusation he turns to his method (11:5–12:13). The Judaizers had been boasting in themselves while discrediting Paul. So Paul will play their game of boasting to make his point (note that in chapters 10–13, the word "boast" and its various forms are used 22 times, and the word "fool" and its other forms are used 7 times). Paul makes nine boasts (he's not actually bragging about himself) to show that he is not inferior to those who seek to discredit him.

Conclusion (12:14–13:14)

- *Paul is coming to visit them* (12:14–13:2). He would come to give, not take. He did not take from them before, and neither did Titus. His letter is designed to prepare them for a joyful visit, but he will deal severely with offenders.
- *He gives another proof of his Apostleship* (13:3-6). That proof is the Corinthians themselves. Thus, they should examine themselves (they were Paul's converts). If they are saved, and they are, it was through Paul!
- *Paul's Desire* (13:7-10). He desires to build them up when he gets to Corinth rather than use sharpness.
- *Closing Exhortation, Benediction Greetings* (13:11-14). Paul had a ministry and he described it (1-7). He had a special duty and he fulfilled it (8-9). He had to defend his ministry and he did it (10-13). Do you have a ministry? How would you describe it? Is it healthy like Paul's or sick like Paul's accusers? Are you responsible for some special duty or project? How is it coming? Is it getting done or being neglected through coldness or procrastination? Is someone accusing you, as they accused Paul, for the purpose of discrediting the good work you are doing for the Lord? How are you handling it? Are you standing firm and courageously against such evil, exposing it for

> **God is able to do far more abundantly than all that we ask or think, according to the power at work within us.**

what it is? Are you praying for God's intervention and deliverance? Remember that God "is able to do far more abundantly than all that we ask or think, according to the power at work within us, to Him be glory in the church and in Christ Jesus throughout all generations, forever and ever. Amen" (Eph. 3:20-21).

THE LETTER TO THE GALATIANS

The Author

According to the salutation, Paul is the author of this letter. He describes himself in Galatians 1:1 as "an apostle—not from men nor through man, but through Jesus Christ and God the Father, who raised Him from the dead." He places a big emphasis on his apostleship. Where did Paul get his apostleship and authority? It was from the risen Christ, not any other source. The Judaizers were denying this by saying that Paul was not sent from God. Paul includes with him in the salutation "and all the brothers who are with me" (1:2a). Paul was probably in Antioch of Syria when he wrote Galatians.

The Readers

Paul sent this letter "to the churches of Galatia" (1:2b). Who were these particular Galatians and where were they located? They were people whom

Paul led to Christ on his first missionary journey (Acts 13–14). Believers in the Galatian cities of Antioch, Iconium, Lystra, Derbe are primarily in mind. You may recall that Timothy was one of Paul's Galatian converts (compare Acts 16:1-4 with 1 Tim. 1:2 where Paul calls him "my true child in the faith"). Paul was persecuted in these cities even to the extent of being stoned and dragged outside the city of Lystra to be left for dead (Acts 14:19), but God raised him up and he went on preaching! He encouraged his converts saying, "Through many tribulations we must enter the kingdom of God" (Acts 14:22). Paul's preaching in Galatia was accompanied by miracle-signs such as the healing of the lame man in Lystra (14:8-10). Elders were appointed in each of the churches and the new believers were commended to the Lord (Acts 14:23). Paul encouraged them to continue in the faith. Unfortunately, some time after Paul left for Antioch, evil Judaizing teachers invaded the churches of Galatia and undermined his apostolic authority and grace teaching. Paul had taught them that they were free from the law for salvation and sanctification. The Judaizing teachers contradicted him by saying that circumcision and law-keeping were essential to salvation and sanctification. Paul sharply rebuked the Galatians ("O foolish Galatians!" Gal. 3:1) for departing from the grace-Gospel he taught them and which they received when he was there.

The Date of Writing Galatians

Scholars are not unanimous on when Paul wrote this important letter. It is the belief of this author that it was about AD 48–49 shortly after Paul evangelized the Galatians.

The Theme of Galatians

Galatians is the charter of Christian liberty. Paul taught the Galatian believers that they were free from the law both for justification and sanctification. However, he equally taught that freedom from the law does not mean one can live a lawless life. However, the believer has the dynamic power of the Holy Spirit to give enablement for holy living (5:16-26).

Paul's Style in Writing Galatians

His style is abrupt and stern due to the nature of their error. They were departing from the grace-Gospel (5:1-6), the only basis of a sinner's standing before God. This awful error must be challenged without ceremony.

Examples of Paul's abrupt speech are found in 1:6-8; 2:11; 3:1-5; 4:12; and 5:12. But notice that Paul is not completely lacking in a loving sensitivity toward them (4:19-20).

The General Structure of Galatians

1. Introduction (1:1-5)
2. Personal Defense (1:6–2:21)
3. Doctrinal Teaching (3:1–5:12)
4. Practical Duties (5:13–6:10)
5. Conclusion (6:11-18)

The Flow of Development of Galatians

1. Introduction (1:1-5)

After confirming that he received his apostleship from none other than Jesus Christ, Paul goes on to wish the Galatian churches "grace" and "peace." This was his usual greeting. However, these terms always have a special application depending on the needs of the readers. The Galatians needed grace to withstand the false teachers who came among them, and grace to hold to the true Gospel. They needed peace—that serenity and calmness of soul—which is the result of totally relying on Christ for salvation and sanctification.

This grace and peace not only comes from the Father, but from His Son, Jesus Christ. What did He do? He "gave Himself for our sins to deliver us from the present evil age." These two clauses tell us that He is the atoning Savior from sin and the delivering Savior from this evil age. He saves and He sanctifies—both on the basis of grace!

2. Paul's Personal Defense (1:6–2:21)

When Paul wrote to various churches he would usually express his thanks for them. He has no thanks for the Galatians! His apostolic message and authority have been attacked so he begins immediately to fight back. He has several important points to make which are meant to set the stage for his doctrinal teaching on justification by faith in Galatians 3:1–5:12.

- *First* (1:6-10), Paul marvels that the Galatian believers were "so quickly deserting Him who called you in the grace of Christ and are turning to a different gospel." He pronounced a curse on any who would preach another Gospel (1:8-9). This is the most severe warning the apostle could give to anyone who would dare pervert the true Gospel. A modern perversion of the Gospel is found in the cults.

- *Secondly* (1:11-24), Paul strongly affirmed that his Gospel was given to him by the Lord Jesus Christ and no one else (1:11-12). What's the evidence? It is Paul's own testimony showing his total independence from others (1:13-24).
- *Thirdly* (2:1-10), Paul says that years later his Gospel was affirmed and defended by the leading men of Jerusalem (James, Cephas, and John). They were not in conflict with Paul and Barnabas. In fact, Paul says, they actually gave to Paul and Barnabas the right hand of fellowship in the preaching of the Gospel to the Gentiles (2:8-9).
- *Fourthly* (2:11-21), Paul successfully defended his Gospel in the face of the hypocrisy of Peter, Barnabas, "the rest of Jews" at Antioch. He testified that his co-crucifixion with Jesus Christ (2:19-21) put an end to the law for salvation and sanctification.

3. Doctrinal Teaching (3:1–5:12)

Affirmation (3:1-18)

Paul affirmed that justification before God is by faith not works of law. He made two points in this regard. First, justification by faith is in keeping with the spiritual experience of the Galatian believers (3:1-5). When Paul preached to them (Acts 13–14), they responded by faith. Law-works had nothing to do with it. Secondly, justification by faith is in keeping with the Old Testament Scriptures. Paul cites the case of Abraham, the father of the Jewish people. How was he justified? He believed the promise of God and it was counted to him for righteousness (3:6-18). Paul also uses Abraham in Romans 4 for the same point. Paul didn't make up the message of justification by faith. This is the way Abraham and all Old Testament believers were justified.

Clarification (3:19–4:7)

Paul did not want his readers to think the law was totally useless. The law is useful and he demonstrates two ways in which this is true. First, (3:19-22) it has the important ministry of revealing sin for what it is—transgression. It condemns the violator (compare Rom. 5:20-21). Secondly, it was a tutor or guardian until the Christ came (3:23–4:7). When the Christ came, the relationship changed from being slaves, circumscribed by the law, to sons of God who are brought into the full liberty of the Holy Spirit and become heirs of God (4:1-7).

Implications (4:8–5:12)

The Galatians did not know the implications of turning to the law for justification before God. It would mean the following six things:

- *First* (4:8-11), it would mean changing one form of bondage (paganism) for another (Judaism).
- *Secondly* (4:12-20), it would mean a rejection of Paul, their spiritual father—one they showed a great deal of affection for when he was among them; on the other hand it would be an acceptance of, and yielding to, dishonest men.
- *Thirdly* (4:21-31), it would mean a great ignorance of the Old Testament. The allegory of the slave woman and the free woman teaches that the two covenants (law and grace) cannot mix.
- *Fourthly* (5:1-6), it would mean that Christ's work on the cross is of no benefit.
- *Fifthly* (5:7-10), it would mean the production of more evil for "a little leaven leavens the whole lump" (5:9).
- *Sixthly* (5:11-12), it would mean that the offence of the cross is removed. If a person can justify themselves by their own works, who will bother them? No one! But tell someone that Jesus is the only way, and that works have nothing to do with justification, and see what happens! You will be labeled a religious fanatic, a narrow bigot.

4. Practical Duties Prescribed by Paul (5:13–6:10)

Being justified by faith has its blessed potential—a life that pleases God in practical matters. Paul gives five practical exhortations which are possible for any believer to fulfill.

- *First* (5:13-15), we are to walk in love. Our new liberty is not to be used as a license to live for self. Love is responsible.
- *Secondly* (5:16-26), we are to walk in the Spirit (see 5:16, 18, 22, 25). This is the opposite of a fleshly life. To walk by the Spirit means

to seek out and follow the Spirit's guidance and help. The Spirit will always lead in agreement with the Word of God.

- *Thirdly* (6:1-5), we are to walk in brotherly responsibility. How? By restoring the weak and bearing one another's burdens.
- *Fourthly* (6:6-9), we are to walk in generosity, supporting God's work and workers. What a person sows they reap. It is an inevitable law. If one sows to the flesh they reap corruption. If one sows to the Spirit—that is, invests one's life in the things of the Holy Spirit—they reap eternal life. Paul encourages not to give up for in due season we shall reap if we do not lose heart.
- *Fifthly* (6:10), we are to walk in goodness toward all men, saved or lost, but especially the saved.

5. Conclusion (6:11-18)

The apostle includes three things in his conclusion:

- *First* (6:11), he authenticates his letter. He wrote it with his own hand as was his custom (see Col. 4:18; Rom. 16:22; 2 Thess. 3:17; 1 Cor. 16:21).
- *Secondly* (6:12-17), he makes his final warning against the Judaizers. There is only one thing to boast in, says Paul, and that is the cross. A ritual, or lack of it, is not important. What is important is a new creation—being born again.
- *Thirdly* (6:18), Paul's benediction brings the epistle to a close. He ends as he began—wishing them grace. What a fitting end!

Galatians teaches us, among other things, that we do not need a law to bind us captive to our Lord. When we trusted Jesus by faith, and put no trust in ourselves or our works, He liberated us by the Holy Spirit so that we might live lives pleasing to Him. What cannot be accomplished in us by the law (justification and sanctification) can be by faith and the ministry of the Holy Spirit. Live in the power of God's liberating grace and Spirit.

> **Live in the power of God's liberating grace and Spirit.**

LESSON 5 EXAM

Use the exam sheet at the back of the book to complete your exam.

1. **Paul wrote 2 Corinthians from**
   A. Asia.
   B. Galatia.
   C. Mysia.
   D. Macedonia.

2. **The theme of 2 Corinthians is the**
   A. apostasy of the last days.
   B. ministry of Paul.
   C. universal church.
   D. gifts of the Holy Spirit.

3. **In 2 Corinthians 4:1-6, Paul's ministry is described as a**
   A. ministry of triumph.
   B. ministry of accreditation.
   C. new covenant ministry.
   D. ministry of honesty.

4. **Incentives to continue in service are**
   A. hope of resurrection.
   B. hope of being in heaven.
   C. hope of rewards.
   D. all of the above.

5. **The duty of Paul's ministry in 2 Corinthians 8–9 was to**
   A. collect material goods for the poor saints in Jerusalem.
   B. organize Gospel teams to preach in each province.
   C. instruct the believers on love for the brethren.
   D. none of the above.

6. **"The churches of Galatia" were those churches founded by**
   A. Peter after he fled from Jerusalem.
   B. Paul on his first missionary journey.
   C. brethren from Lystra and Derbe.
   D. Barnabas along with John Mark.

7. **The theme of Galatians is**
   A. the rapture of the church to heaven.
   B. Christian liberty.
   C. the doctrine of redemption.
   D. the resurrection of Jesus Christ.

8. **Paul's style in writing Galatians was**
   A. abrupt and stern.
   B. matter of fact and informational.
   C. gentle and humble.
   D. serene and joyous.

9. **Paul's teaching in 6:7 was given in the context of**
   A. being generous in giving to the Lord's work.
   B. sexual immorality.
   C. lying and stealing.
   D. forsaking the meetings of the church.

10. **Paul taught the Galatians to boast only in**
    A. success in evangelism.
    B. being correct in doctrine.
    C. being virtuous in living.
    D. the cross.

What Do You Say?

What evidence is there in your life of the presence of the Holy Spirit? Explain.

Ephesians and Philippians

Background Information

The Prison Epistles consist of Ephesians, Philippians, Colossians, and Philemon. They are brief in length in comparison to the books we have so far surveyed. However, their brevity does not mean they are less significant. Actually, some of the most wonderful truths concerning Christ and the church are found in these four letters. Before we survey these letters, let us become familiar with seven questions of a background nature:

How do we know that Paul was in prison when he wrote these letters?

The answer is that he refers to himself as such 15 times (Eph. 3:1,13; 4:1; 6:20; Phil. 1:7, 13, 14, 17; Col. 4:3, 10, 18; Philem. 1:1, 9, 10, 23).

Where was Paul imprisoned when he wrote these letters?

He was in Rome. How do we know? Observe the mention of the household of Caesar and the Praetorium Guard (Phil. 1:13; 4:22).

What are the general facts of his imprisonment?

He was captured in Jerusalem after the third journey (Acts 21–23). He was transferred to Caesarea a short time later and imprisoned there for two years (Acts 23–26). Then he was sent to Rome by ship (Acts 27–28). He was in custody in Rome for two years living in his own rented house, but in chains (Acts 28:16, 30).

What was Paul's activity while in prison?

He received Christians and non-Christians (compare Acts 28:17-31). He taught the Gospel to those who visited him. Even the Roman guards to whom the apostle was chained heard the good news and some of them were saved. This is probably how the Gospel got into Caesar's household (Phil. 1:13). And, of course, he wrote the Prison Epistles!

What was Paul's attitude while in prison?

Paul was very positive. In Philippians, for instance, he manifested great joy, victory, trust, and confidence. In Ephesians, he calls himself a prisoner of the Lord which shows the attitude of submission to God's sovereignty.

What were Paul's prospects for the future?

He knew he would be released and have further ministry (Phil. 1:19-30). His second Roman imprisonment did not have this prospect (2 Tim. 4:4-6).

What practical lessons can be learned from Paul's prison experience?

- Trials can be a great benefit to one's self, as well as others. Others were encouraged by Paul (Phil. 1:1-14).
- God is greater than our circumstances and sufficient for our needs (Phil. 4:13).
- Be preoccupied with being a servant in whatever situation in life (Eph. 6:19-20).
- Remember that to the Christian, nothing happens by chance. Paul was a prisoner of the Lord, not Rome (Eph. 3:1, 13)!
- The grass is always greener on your side of the fence when you are in, and doing, the will of God. Paul did not complain or develop bitterness.
- Lifetime is training time for reigning time! Do not despise the chastening of the Lord for it is beneficial to us (Prov. 3:11-12).
- View everything through the eyes of our heavenly Father. Some of the best and most lasting things, spiritually, come through adversity.

THE LETTER TO THE EPHESIANS

Background

The city of Ephesus was located on the western coast of the province of Asia on the banks of the Cayster River. Its port was Miletus. Ephesus was the capital of Asia. Today it is a small Turkish town called Anasaluk. Many ruins are visible such as the remains of an amphitheater referred to in Acts 19:29. The inhabitants were a mixture of Greeks, Romans, and Jewish. It was a very rich commercial city—the best in Asia Minor. Paganism was very strong. The worship of Artemis (called Diana by the Romans) was predominant. The temple of Artemis was one of the ancient wonders of the world. Its size was 425 by 240 feet. It had massive columns which rose 60 feet. The temple building, measuring 343 by 164 feet was supported by 100 of these columns. In the inner shrine was an image of Artemis. It was believed that this image had fallen from heaven (Acts 19:35).

Judaism was well established in Ephesus. There was a synagogue there which was the only witness to monotheism (belief in one God). Paul boldly ministered to the Jewish people. Acts 19:8-9 says that he preached over a three-month period of time and was forced to find another place—the school of Tyrannus—in which to minister the Gospel. Why? Because the Jewish people resisted his reasoning and persuasion, bringing persecution.

God authenticated the message he preached by granting special miracles (Acts 19:11-12). Many believed. Those who had been involved in Satanic magic burned their books in the sight of all as an evidence of the genuineness of their conversion (Acts 19:18-20). More persecution broke out. This time it was from the pagans who were losing economically due to the success of the Gospel (Acts 19:21-41). Paul eventually had to leave (Acts 20:1), but not before he had spent over three years there and had established a spiritually strong church.

The Author of Ephesians

According to Ephesians 1:1, it was "Paul, an apostle of Jesus Christ by the will of God." He mentions his name again in 3:1 and the fact that he is a "prisoner" in 4:1.

The Readers of Ephesians

Ephesians 1:1 describes the Ephesians as "saints ... and faithful in Christ Jesus." The word "saints" speaks of the position these believers had before God as holy. There is just one requirement to be a saint—faith in Jesus! In other words, every believer stands before God as a saint. The word "faithful" tells us that they were living the life of faith and holiness. The spiritual and moral condition of one's life should match his position (standing) before God.

Date of Writing Ephesians

This was sometime between AD 60 and 62 when Paul was imprisoned in Rome. This date is true for the other three prison letters.

Some Points of Interest

Ephesians is very universal in nature, putting an emphasis on the whole body of Christ, not just a local church. Secondly, it is non-controversial. That is, it is not a book which was produced by Paul to solve church problems like 1 Corinthians was. Thirdly, it has many parallels in Colossians. In fact, 78 of the 95 verses in Colossians are similar to Ephesians. Fourthly, there are two key expressions. One is "in Christ" which speaks not only of our union with Him, but also our position of acceptance. The other is "in the heavenlies" (ESV reads "heavenly places"). The "heavenlies" is the realm of the unseen kingdom of God. It is the sphere of spiritual reality where we live and move and have our being spiritually. We get into "the heavenlies" by means of the new birth (John 3). The expression is used five times in Ephesians (1:3; 1:20; 2:6; 3:10; 6:12). In 1:3, it is the realm of all our spiritual blessings. In 1:20 and 2:6, it is the sphere where Christ reigns and

> **There is just one requirement to be a saint—faith in Jesus!**

His people reign with Him. In 3:10 and 6:12, it is a realm where spirit beings—good and evil—continue to operate. We must be careful not to equate "the heavenlies" with heaven. One reason for that is the fact that it is a realm where there is conflict and that is not true of heaven. The heavenlies, though an invisible and unseen realm, is just as real as the "earthlies" in which we live by our senses. In a way, the believer lives in both realms, but God wants the heavenly to dominate the earthly (compare Col. 3:1-2).

The Theme of Ephesians

When one reads the letter to the Ephesians he is reading about God's wonderful creation of the church universal. The theme is the Church as the Body of Christ. The truth of the church was a revelation made known to Paul (Eph. 3:3-7). It was a mystery in the sense that it was not revealed in the Old Testament.

The General Structure of Ephesians

1. The Doctrine Concerning the Universal Church (1:1–3:21)
2. The Duties of the Universal Church (4:1–6:24)

The Flow of Development of Ephesians

Now let's look more closely at the two sections described above.

1. The Doctrine Concerning the Universal Church (1:1–3:21)

Praise for the Churches' Spiritual Blessings in Christ (1:1-14)

The whole Trinity—Father, Son, and Holy Spirit—are involved in salvation. First, the Father chose us in Christ before the foundation of the world, and He predestined us to adoption as sons in His great family (1:3-6). Secondly, the Son's part was to redeem and forgive us, give us insight into God's will, and assure an inheritance to us (1:7-12). Thirdly, the Holy Spirit became the seal of our security in Christ, and the pledge of our future inheritance in heaven (1:13-14). We are indeed very wealthy in spiritual blessings (1:3)—the kind that count throughout eternity!

Prayer for the Churches' Spiritual Enlightenment in Christ (1:15-23)

The Ephesians needed enlightenment so that they might know three things. First, Paul says, I want you to "know what is the hope to which He has called you" (1:18). This refers to their being in heaven and enjoying their inheritance. What a wonderful hope. Secondly, he wants them to know "what are the riches of His glorious inheritance in the saints" (1:18). They not only have an inheritance from God, but God has an inheritance in them! That means that believers then, and now, are a treasure of incomparable worth to Him! Thirdly, he wants them to know "what is the immeasurable greatness of His power toward us who believe" (1:19). In the

Old Testament, there are many witnesses to God's great power. One was the creation. Another was the exodus from Egypt. In the New Testament, God's great power is manifested in the resurrection, ascension, exaltation, and dominion of Jesus Christ (1:19-23). Knowing these three things should be a great incentive to live a strong and devoted life for Jesus Christ.

The Proclamation of the Churches' Spiritual Perspective in Christ (2:1–3:20)

Having the right perspective on something is often the reason for success rather than failure. This is very true in spiritual matters. The perspective Paul gives us in these two chapters should make us true worshipers and enthusiastic servants of Christ. Note all the new things we have in Christ:

- *A new life (2:1-5).* We once were dead in sin.
- *A new position (2:6).* We are raised up and seated with Him in the heavenlies.
- *A new prospect (2:7).* We shall be monuments of God's grace forever in heaven.
- *A new basis for salvation (2:8-9).* We are saved by grace through faith.
- *A new calling and responsibility (2:10).* To good works.
- *A new community (2:11-18).* Jewish people and Gentiles forming one new man.
- *A new destiny (2:19-22).* A dwelling of God in the Spirit.
- *A new revelation (3:1-13).* That Gentiles should be fellow heirs, of the same body, and partakers of His promise in Christ by the Gospel.
- *A new enablement (3:14-21).* Strengthened with might by His Spirit in the inner man.

2. The Duties of the Universal Church (4:1-6:24)

With Paul, doctrine and duty go together. Doctrine is the basis for duty. Duty is result of doctrine. Paul views this duty in the church, society, the home, and the spiritual battleground.

Duty in the Church—Be Unified (4:1-16)

Paul makes an appeal for unity, calling upon believers to walk in a manner worthy of our calling. This kind of walk is characterized by humility, gentleness, patience, bearing with one another, and love (4:1-3). The basis for such a unity is the seven-fold unity of the church (4:4-6). The means to promote and maintain unity in the church is the giving of gifted men to the church "to equip the saints for the work of ministry, for building up the body of Christ" (4:7-16). There is no reason why this duty of unity cannot be powerfully achieved. In unity there is power.

Duty in Society—Watch How You Live (4:17–5:21)

The word "walk" in Ephesians is a key word. It is used as a metaphor of an ordered course of life—the way one habitually lives or should live. Ephesians tells us how not to walk (live habitually), as well as how we should live. First, Paul calls all to a walk in newness of life (4:17–5:2). This means, for instance, that the old life-style of lying, unrighteous anger, stealing, corrupt communication, etc., are to be taken off, as one would remove a filthy garment, and replaced by a clean garment of positive virtues. Negative attitudes and speaking are to be put away and replaced with tenderheartedness and forgiveness. We are to "walk in love, as Christ also has loved us." This standard of love is very high, but God's commands are His enablings. Believers have the Holy Spirit and thus the ability to fulfill His love.

Secondly, we are called upon to protect the Christian fellowship (5:3-6). Paul gives a strong exhortation against allowing an evil life-style in the church—immoral acts and words. The church's reputation is at stake.

Thirdly, Paul exhorts believers to "walk as children of light" (5:7-14). This involves on the one hand manifesting the positive fruit of the Spirit, which consists of "all that is good and right and true," and on the other hand of having the courage of not only not participating in evil but actually exposing evil for what it is—"the unfruitful works of darkness." Fourthly, Paul calls upon the Ephesians, and us, to "look carefully then how you walk, not as unwise but as wise," (5:15-17). In the context, walking wisely has to do with the redeeming (conserving) of our time. How, according to Paul, does one redeem the time? "Understand what the will of the Lord is," is Paul's instruction.

> **Believers have the Holy Spirit and thus the ability to fulfill Christ's love.**

Fifthly, Paul commands believers to "not get drunk with wine, for that is debauchery, but be filled with the Spirit" (5:18-20). To be filled with the Spirit is to be controlled by the Holy Spirit. The results of being filled are given in verses 19-21. If one wants to know if he/she is filled (controlled) by the Holy Spirit, just observe what Paul gives as evidence of filling and see if it matches one's life.

Duty in the Home (5:22–6:9)

This section is really a continuation of the section on Spirit-filling. The connection is found in the word "submitting" (5:21). A Spirit-filled (controlled) family (wives-husbands, children-parents, servants-masters) will manifest submission. By way of application, the intact spiritual family will make an impact outside the home—neighborhood, school, workplace, church, etc.

Duty on the Battlefield—Christian Warfare (6:10-20)

Sooner or later every believer discovers that the Christian life is a battleground, not a playground, and that they face an enemy who is much stronger than they are. How can the believer win the battle against the devil? Only in God's strength. Our enemy is not only powerful but also cunning and crafty and he has an army of demonic spirits to do his bidding throughout the world. There is only one way to defeat him: "Be strong in the Lord and in the strength of His might. Put on the whole armor of God, that you may be able to stand against the schemes of the devil" (6:10-11). Paul uses the armor of a Roman soldier as the imagery to convey the spiritual armor which every believer needs in the battle. It would be a familiar illustration to anyone living in the Roman empire. The armor is both moral and spiritual—truth, righteousness, Gospel preparedness, faith, hope of salvation, and God's word. Every army needs a communications system to keep it in contact with headquarters. For the believer, prayer is that communication system: "praying at all times in the Spirit, with all prayer and supplication. To that end, keep alert with all perseverance, making supplication for all the saints" (6:18). Paul is one of those saints and so he asks that they pray for him (6:19-20) that he might be bold in proclaiming the Gospel.

> **If Jesus Christ loved the church and gave Himself for it, then we should love it too and give ourselves in selfless sacrifice.**

Conclusion 6:21-24

He concludes by informing that he is sending Tychicus, a beloved brother, to let them know how Paul is doing; also he will comfort their hearts (6:21-22). He pronounces a benediction wishing them peace, love, faith, and grace. These are ingredients to powerful living for Christ.

As believers we may never have wealth, rank, or station in this life. But

EPHESIANS AND PHILIPPIANS **103**

we should never forget that we are in Christ and thus incredibly wealthy in spiritual blessings. We also are members of the church, the Body of Christ. All earthly organization and human movements pale into insignificance in the light of the glory of this great body with Christ as the Head. We should never forget that "Christ loved the church and gave Himself up for her, that He might sanctify her, having cleansed her by the washing of water with the word, so that He might present the church to Himself in splendor, without spot or wrinkle or any such thing, that she might be holy and without blemish" (5:25-27). If Jesus Christ loved the church and gave Himself for it, then we should love it too and give ourselves in selfless sacrifice through all the days the Lord gives us on this earth. Concerning the local church you should ask yourself this question: "If every church member were just like me, what kind of a church would my church be?"

THE LETTER TO THE PHILIPPIANS

Background

The city of Philippi was in the province of Macedonia located on the frontier of Europe and Asia. Because of its location, it was an important city militarily. The port city of Neapolis was its outlet to the sea. It got its name from Philip II, the father of Alexander the Great. The city was occupied mostly by Romans and Greeks. There were just a few Jewish people.

Like Corinth, it was a Roman colony, becoming such in 42 BC. As you may remember, a Roman colony was a free city—a little bit of Rome away from Rome, having the same rights and liberty. It is possible that Paul made a play on words (pun) in Philippians 3:20 when in one translation he called the Philippian believers "a colony of heaven."

The church in Philippi was started by Paul on the second missionary journey (Acts 16:11-40). When Paul began the second journey (Acts 16:1-11) he went over some old ground, strengthening churches which he started on the first journey. Eventually he came to Troas where he had a night vision. In the vision, he saw a man from Macedonia pleading with him to "come over to Macedonia and help us." He took that as the guidance of God and left immediately from Troas for Macedonia.

On the first Sabbath day Paul went to the riverside where a group of women were praying. There was no synagogue in Philippi. Paul preached to the women. One of them, Lydia, trusted the Lord and was baptized (Acts 16:11-15). Paul's next encounter was with a demon-possessed girl whose masters had profited greatly from her. When they saw that their hope of profit was gone, they were furious. They had Paul and Silas beaten with many stripes and thrown into prison (16:16-24). At midnight, Paul and Silas were praying and singing hymns to God, and the prisoners were listening to them (16:25-34). An earthquake caused the prison doors to open and the chains of the prisoners fell off. The jailer tried to kill himself but was stopped by Paul and Silas. He asked, "What must I do to be saved?" And they said, "Believe in the Lord Jesus Christ, and you will be saved ...." After being released from prison, Paul went to the house of Lydia before departing from the city (Acts 16:35-40). The church in Philippi was one of the dearest and most loved churches founded by Paul. The letter to the Philippians shows the loving heart of Paul toward these believers.

The Author of Philippians

According to Philippians 1:1, Paul wrote this letter. He included Timothy in the salutation with him, and mentions him again in chapter 2 as an example of selflessness.

The Readers of Philippians

The letter is addressed to "all the saints in Christ Jesus who are at Philippi, with the overseers and deacons." We have already mentioned that the word "saints" is a term reflecting our position before God as holy. The church leaders—overseers and deacons—are specifically addressed. Overseers (sometimes translated "bishops") are also called "elders" in the New Testament. Overseer refers to their work and elder to their spiritual maturity.

The Date of Writing Philippians

This is the same as Ephesians. Sometime between AD 60 and 62.

The Occasion for Writing Philippians

In Christian love, the Philippian church had sent a gift of fellowship to Paul to help meet his needs. This gift was brought to Paul by Epaphroditus who was a leader in the Philippian church. Paul was touched by such love and shares his feelings about it in 4:12-20. Expressing his thanks, then, became the occasion to write to them about others things as well.

The Key Word of Philippians—Joy

The word "joy" and its various forms (rejoice, rejoicing, etc.) are found as a noun seven times and as a verb nine times in the letter (1:4, 18, 25; 2:2, 17, 18, 28; 3:1; 4:1, 4, 10). It was joy that filled Paul's life in difficult circumstances and he wished this same joy for the Philippians (4:4). Happiness depends on what happens. Joy, in contrast, is not dependent on circumstance. Joy is one of the fruits of the Holy Spirit (Gal. 5:22). Therefore, any believer can have Christian joy.

A Chief Characteristic of Philippians

This letter is very personal and practical. Paul really loved these believers and his warmth and tenderness often shine through. He has great praise for Epaphroditus, their messenger, and he has fond remembrance of their help, kindness, and sacrifice.

The General Structure of Philippians

1. Introduction (1:1-11)
2. Information (1:12-26)
3. Exhortation (1:27–2:30)
4. Admonition (3:1-21)
5. Encouragement (4:1-9)
6. Conclusion (4:10-23)

The Flow of Development of Philippians

1. Introduction (1:1-11)

After the salutation (1:1-2), the apostle expresses his thanks to God for the Philippian believers, especially for their participation with him in the spread of the Gospel (1:3-8). They are a loving church but there is always room for growth in this virtue. So he prays that their love might increase and abound in the areas of knowledge and discernment. The blessed results of such an intelligent discerning love are both for now and later (1:9-11).

2. Information (1:12-26)

People who love us are always concerned when we are in trouble. They want to know how we are doing so as to pray more intelligently for us and help us in any way possible. Paul is in trouble and wants to pass on to the Philippians information on how he is handling his situation. He shares two things which would be of encouragement to them. First, he is *conquering* in his adversity. The Gospel is spreading still more since his imprisonment (1:12-18). Secondly, he is *confident* in his adversity (1:19-26). He has no doubt that he will be released from his imprisonment (see 1:19, 25; 2:24). Someone has said that every wind of adversity is just another vote of confidence from God. Adversity causes us to send our spiritual roots down deeply into Him. Paul experienced this!

3. Exhortation (1:27–2:30)

The exhortations in this long section concern pressures from without (1:27-30) and problems from within (2:1-30). The first exhortation is "only let your manner of life be worthy of the Gospel of Christ." How may they do this? By being unified and fearless in the preaching of the Gospel (1:27-28), and by understanding that sufferings are normal for believers (1:29-30).

The second exhortation (2:1-30) is to be humble and submissive, looking out for the needs of others as well as your own (2:1-4). Paul gives four examples of this kind of humble, submissive, and selfless spirit. Observe them:

- *Jesus Christ (2:5-16).* He is the supreme, ultimate example. This One who was "in the form of God, did not count equality with God a thing to be grasped, but emptied himself, by taking the form of a servant, being born in the likeness of men." As a man He was obedient unto death, even death on the cross. Jesus was concerned about others and we are to have the same attitude.

  Jesus was concerned about others and we are to have the same attitude.

- *The Apostle Paul (2:17-18).* Paul, like his Lord and Savior, lived for others. His deep humility is seen when he compares the faith of the Philippians with his own. To do this he uses the imagery of the Old Testament sacrifices. He looked upon the sacrifice and service of the Philippians as comparable to the burnt offering (Ex. 20:24), and saw his own service of faith as just the small drink offering (Lev. 23:13) which was poured over the burnt offering. Is this the perspective we have as we serve alongside other believers?

- *Timothy (2:19-24)*. Paul commended him for his selfless and sensitive spirit in the care of other believers. As far as Paul was concerned, there was no other associate so like-minded in shepherding others (2:20-21).
- *Epaphroditus (2:25-30)*. Paul says of him that "for the work of Christ, he came close to death, not regarding his life" (2:30). His motto was: "I will live, not for myself, but for others!" Is this your motto?

4. Admonition (3:1-21)

One way Satan sought to infiltrate the early church was through false prophets and teachers. False teaching had not yet reached Philippi, but Paul envisioned it happening. Thus he warned of the coming of these evil men. Paul made the following points:

- *False Teachers Characterized (3:1-2)*. They are dogs, speaking of their unclean nature. They are evil workers, speaking of their evil activity. They are those who mutilate the flesh, speaking of their false doctrine of circumcision which they tried to impose on believers as a requirement for salvation. They taught that the sacrifice of Christ on the cross was not sufficient for them. Law works were necessary, too.
- *False Teachers Contrasted with True Believers (3:3)*. Paul says that the true believer worships God in Spirit, not ritual. The believer's focus is Christ Jesus in whom they rejoice, not law-works, and they have no confidence in fleshly efforts to please God.
- *False Teachers Compared to Paul (3:4-16)*. Whether in Judaism (3:4-6), in present salvation (4:7-11), or the future prospect of the believer (3:12-16), the false teachers could not hold a candle to Paul.
- *The False Teachers Condemned (3:17-21)*. They are called "enemies of the cross of Christ" which means that these lawless individuals hate God's grace. Their "end is destruction" which tells us that they are on the way to hell. Their "god is their belly" which demonstrates that their appetite is greed. They "glory in their shame" instead of the Christ and His cross. They have "minds set on [preoccupied with] earthly things." All these false teachers have is what their senses can communicate. But true believers do not find a lasting home in this world. Their citizenship is in heaven and they are waiting for the Savior to come and take them there (3:20-21)!

5. Encouragement (4:1-9)

Paul encourages in six practical areas. He exhorts to unity in the church. Two sisters are out of harmony with one another and need to get back into fellowship so that the work is not hindered (4:1-3). He encourages to joyfulness (4:4), gentleness (4:5), trust in God through prayer and supplication (4:6-7), a quality thought life (4:8), and a quality lifestyle (4:9). The lack of these virtues makes for great weakness and ineffectiveness in one's personal life and in the church.

6. Conclusion (4:10-23)

Paul closes the letter by acknowledging the Philippians' gift (4:10-20), by giving greetings from brethren who are with him (4:21-22), and by wishing them the "grace of the Lord Jesus Christ" (4:23).

What kind of church is your church? There is much to be commended and followed in the Philippian church. They had a good leadership (1:1 with 2:25, 30), they were a serving church (1:3-8), they were a loving church (1:9-11), and generous church, etc. (4:15-16). Every church should do a self-evaluation on a regular basis. Each church should ask itself tough questions about its spiritual and moral condition. If there is a need to change then determine to make the adjustments. There was a need for some change in the Philippian church and Paul, through this letter, sought to help them accomplish this. Maybe this letter will be a help to you in the making of needed changes.

LESSON 6 EXAM

Use the exam sheet at the back of the book to complete your exam.

1. **The predominant idol worship in Ephesus was the worship**
    A. of Baal.   C. of Astarte.
    B. of Zeus.   D. of Artemis.

2. **Paul called the Ephesian believers "saints," which means**
    A. they were living holy lives.
    B. their position before God was holy.
    C. that they were considered the best church.
    D. that they had a special place in the church.

3. **Paul's first prayer for the Ephesians was for spiritual**
    A. power in Christ.
    B. enlightenment in Christ.
    C. love in Christ.
    D. enthusiasm in Christ.

4. **Paul commanded the Ephesian believers to be**
    A. indwelt by the Holy Spirit.
    B. baptized with the Holy Spirit.
    C. filled with the Holy Spirit.
    D. sealed with the Spirit.

5. **The armor which Paul exhorts all believers to wear is both**
    A. moral and spiritual.
    B. religious and ethical.
    C. religious and moral.
    D. spiritual and religious.

6. **The city of Philippi was an important city**
    A. religiously.   C. politically.
    B. militarily.   D. commercially.

7. **Paul's occasion for writing Philippians was the fact that**
    A. the church was invaded by false teachers.
    B. a gift had been sent to Paul by the Philippians.
    C. Lydia had died.
    D. Paul was planning a visit to them.

8. **The key word of Philippians is**
    A. holy.   C. peace.
    B. love.   D. joy.

9. **Paul said that the adversity he was experiencing in his imprisonment (1:12-26) was causing him to be both**
    A. downcast yet rejoicing.
    B. joyful though without hope.
    C. conquering and confident.
    D. displeased and resigned to his fate.

10. **One whom Paul used as an example of a humble, submissive, and selfless person was**
    A. Epaphroditus.   C. Peter.
    B. Silas.   D. Barnabas.

What Do You Say?

What was Paul's attitude towards his imprisonment, and how can this be an encouragement to you?

_____

_____

_____

_____

Colossians and Philemon

THE LETTER TO THE COLOSSIANS

Background

The city of Colossae was located in the Roman province of Asia about 100 miles east of Ephesus. It was an important city in the fifth century BC. However, in New Testament times it was small in size and of very low rank and importance. It was near the cities of Hierapolis and Laodicea mentioned in 4:13. The origin of the name of the city is uncertain. One speculation is that Colossae relates to the word *colossus,* which stands for the fantastic shapes of rock formations found there.

Paul had never visited Colossae prior to the time he wrote this epistle. This seems to be the inference in 2:1, where he speaks of those who have not seen his face in the flesh. How, then, did the church there get started? One theory is that Epaphras, mentioned in 1:7 and 4:12, evangelized the Colossians and started the church. This view speculates that Paul won Epaphras to the Lord while he was evangelizing in Ephesus (Acts 19), and that Epaphras was challenged to carry the Gospel to his home town. This is altogether possible.

Epaphras informed Paul of the faith, hope, and love of the Colossians. He was a man with a shepherd-heart for the believers in Colossae and prayed earnestly that they might stand "mature and fully assured in all the will of God" (4:12). It appears from Philemon 1:2-3 that the church had its meetings in the house of Philemon. To this small and seemingly insignificant church, living in a comparatively insignificant city, was written some of the great truths about the person and work of Christ!

The Author and Readers

Like Ephesians and Philippians, this letter was written by Paul from his Roman imprisonment. Once again, Timothy is included in the salutation (1:1). The Colossian believers are described as "saints and faithful brethren in Christ."

The Bearer of the Letter

Tychicus (4:7) carried the letter to Colossae. Paul said this brother would inform them of all the news about him, and that he would find out their circumstances and comfort their hearts. Onesimus, the runaway slave of Philemon, would be with him.

The Date of Writing

Colossians was written in the same time-frame as Ephesians and Philippians. That is somewhere between AD 60 and 62.

The Theme of the Letter

The theme of this letter of 95 verses is both doctrinal and practical. It has an emphasis on the supremacy of Christ in His person and work in the first two chapters. Chapters three and four deal with practical Christian living.

Two Points of Interest

Of the 95 verses in Colossians, 78 are similar to Ephesians. Try reading Colossians immediately after Ephesians and you will be impressed with its great similarity.

> In Colossians, the emphasis is on Christ's exalted position over the church as its head.

Secondly, there is an emphasis on the person and work of Christ. Jesus is "the beloved Son" (1:13), the redeemer (1:14), "the image of the invisible God" (1:15a), "the firstborn of all creation" (1:15b), the Creator (1:16), the pre-existent One (1:17a), the Sustainer (1:17b), "the head of the body" (1:18a), "the firstborn from the dead" (1:18b), and God who is the head over all rule and authority (2:9-10). The description of Jesus as "the head of the body" (the church) is the key feature of Christ's person emphasized in the letter. In Ephesians, the emphasis is on the "church, which is His body" (Eph. 1:22-23). In Colossians, the emphasis is on Christ's exalted position over the church as its head. Evidently the Colossians were being troubled by false teachers who were promoting heresy concerning Christ's person and work. Paul counters with the truth about Jesus—truth which is still being used today by true believers to counter the false teaching of modern day cults. The true identity of Jesus is so clear in Colossians that some cults, who hate the truth, have sought to change it by their own translations.

The General Structure of Colossians

1. The Introduction (1:1-14)
2. The Preeminent Christ (1:15–2:5)
3. The Threat of Heresy (2:6-23)
4. Practical Exhortations (3:1–4:6)
5. Conclusion (4:7-18)

The Flow of Development of Colossians

1. The Introduction (1:1-14)

The introduction consist of three parts. The first is the salutation (1:1-2). The second is Paul's thanksgiving to God for salvation, which the Colossians have experienced as evidenced in their faith, love, and hope (1:3-8). The third is Paul's prayer for the Colossian believers that they might be "filled with the knowledge of His will in all spiritual wisdom and understanding" (1:9-14). With this spiritual knowledge (divine revelation), they will be able to properly live for God and be protected from error.

2. The Preeminent Christ (1:15-2:5)

This one who is the "image of the invisible God" has headship (authority) in three areas: He is head over creation (1:15b-17), over the church (1:18a), and in resurrection. The term "firstborn" does not have to do with physical relationship in these verses. Rather, it refers metaphorically to rank, supremacy, and uniqueness. For instance, Jesus was the firstborn from the dead, in the sense that He was the first to rise from the dead never to die again. Because Jesus is God, He was able to effect reconciliation through His death on the cross (1:19-23).

The preeminent human servant to proclaim this message to the Gentile world was the apostle Paul (1:24-2:5). Paul gives six facets of his ministry as an apostle:

- *Description of it*—A Ministry of Suffering (1:24)
- *Origin of it*—A Stewardship from God (1:25)
- *Message-content of it*—"Christ in you, the Hope of Glory" (1:26-28a)
- *Purpose of it*—To Present Everyone Complete in Christ (1:28b)
- *Manner of it*—Labor … Striving According to God's Power (1:29)
- *Concern of it*—Encouragement in and Preservation of Faith (2:1-5)

3. The Threat of Heresy (2:6-23)

The Preventatives for Heresy (2:6-15)

Before actually describing the heresy, Paul gives three preventative safeguards. The first is to walk in Christ in fellowship and obedience (2:6-7). The second is to be on the alert, to be diligent. Do not be taken captive through human philosophy (2:8). The third is establishment in the truth (2:9-15). The Lord Jesus Christ is God. You are complete in Him. You have experienced complete identification with Christ in His death, burial, and resurrection! You need nothing else. You have the truth as it is in Jesus.

The Identification of the Heresy (2:16-23)

Three heresies are identified by Paul. The first is legalism. This is an attempt to gain favor with God by human efforts (2:16-17). The second is mysticism consisting of a false humility, the worship of angels and intruding into those things which one has not seen (2:18-19). This may have been for the arrogant purpose of obtaining some deeper or secret knowledge not available to the legitimate apostles (as the Gnostics claimed to have). The third heresy is a false asceticism (mistreatment of the physical body) which consists of an unbiblical self-denial of things which are actually legitimate (2:20-23). This type of practice may appear to be wise and humble but it has no value in quenching the lusts of the sinful nature. God's way is working from the inside out. Religious asceticism is the opposite.

> **The heresy of legalism is an attempt to gain favor with God by human efforts.**

4. Practical Exhortations (3:1–4:6)

Paul, as he usually does in his writings, goes from doctrine to practical Christian living. The first is the basis for the second. The section develops with exhortation to all believers (3:1-17), then exhortation to the Christian household (3:18–4:1), and then back to exhortation for all (4:2-6).

Exhortation to All the Believers (3:1-17)

He makes a general appeal to have a strong and continuous spiritual focus on things above and not on things of the earth (3:1-2). He gives three strong incentives for being heavenly-minded, spiritual Christians (3:3-4). These are our past identification with Christ in His death and resurrection (3:3a), our present preservation with Christ in God (3:3b), and our future glorification with Christ at the Second Coming (3:4).

> **Paul appeals us to have a strong and continuous spiritual focus on things above and not on things of the earth.**

Having made the general appeal for spirituality, he now calls upon the Colossians to put out of their lives the immoral things which once characterized them (3:5-11), and take on a virtuous life-style with a determination to let God's peace rule in their hearts and Christ's Word dwell in them richly in all wisdom (3:12-17).

Exhortation to the Christian Household (3:18–4:1)

Domestic relationships are emphasized here. This is the same as Ephesians 5:20-6:9, although it is only half as long. It consists of teaching concerning wives and husbands (3:18-19), children and parents (3:20-21), and slaves and masters (3:22–4:1). These exhortations have never become outdated. They are still needed today in the community of believers as they were in Paul's day!

Exhortation to All Believers (4:2-6)

There are three exhortations given. The first is to devotedness to prayer (4:2-4). They are to be alert and thankful in their prayer life and to be sure to pray for Paul for an open door of evangelism. Secondly, they are to be wise in their conduct before the lost (4:5). Thirdly, they must be gracious and honest in their speech (4:6). Just think of the influence Christians would have in this world if these three exhortations were consistently obeyed.

5. Conclusion (4:7-18)

The conclusion has variety. After saying that Tychicus would inform the Colossians about Paul's situation (4:7-9), he goes on to give greetings from his associates (4:10-15), instruction concerning the reading and sharing of this letter (4:16), and warning to Archippus to be responsible as a servant of the Lord (4:17). He then makes an appeal that they remember his imprisonment (4:18a)—inferring that they should pray for him in it—and closes the letter by wishing them grace (1:18b).

Paul's final wish of grace for the Colossians is not just empty words. Without God's grace we would still be in our sins. Without God's grace we would be weak and powerless as Christians. We need God's grace every day, and He has assured us that we can come with confidence to the throne of grace to find grace to help in time of need (Heb. 4:16).

THE LETTER TO PHILEMON

This brief letter actually comes after Titus in our New Testament. Chronologically, however, it is one of the prison epistles and so we consider it here.

The Author and Readers of Philemon

According to 1:1, Paul was the author of this brief letter. He includes Timothy with him in the salutation. He does not mention his apostleship or servanthood as he normally does in the salutations of his letters. He simply identifies himself as a prisoner of Christ Jesus. He refers to his prisoner-status three more times (1:10, 13, 23).

His primary reader is Philemon whom he described as "beloved" and "a fellow worker." The fact that Paul made a request of Philemon shows that he was the prime reader. Secondarily he addressed Apphia, Archippus, and the church in his house.

The Date of Writing

Philemon was written at the same time as the other three prison letters—somewhere between AD 60 and 62.

The Bearer of the Letter

Philemon and Colossians were most certainly sent at the same time. The bearer of the Colossian epistle (Tychicus) most assuredly carried this one as well.

The Occasion for Writing

The occasion was the return of Philemon's runaway slave, Onesimus (1:10-13). Paul had met this man in Rome during his imprisonment. He led him to Christ ("whose father I became in my imprisonment," 1:10).

The Purpose for Writing

The letter has two purposes. First, Paul wanted to secure reconciliation between Philemon and Onesimus (1:8-21). Secondly, he asks for lodging (which shows that Paul envisioned being set free from prison, 1:22).

Information on Onesimus and Philemon

Onesimus' name means useful or profitable. Paul makes a play on his name in 1:11. His status was that of a bondslave (1:16). His crimes were running away (punishable by death if Philemon wanted to), and he had wronged Philemon in some way (1:18).

Philemon's name means loving. Verse 19 may infer that Paul was instrumental in leading him to the Lord. Paul considered him a fellow-laborer, and a man of good testimony (1:5). He was also very close to Paul ("partner," 1:17).

The Key Expression in the Letter

The key expression is "receive Him" (1:12, 15, 17). Paul wants Philemon to receive Onesimus back into his household. He does not use his apostolic authority to demand of Philemon to take Onesimus. Rather, in verses 9-21 he tactfully, and with grace, attempts to move Philemon to act in a gracious and forgiving manner. We do not know if Philemon did so, but it is hard to believe that he could resist the beautiful and powerful persuasion of Paul.

Slavery was an institution in the ancient world. There were millions of slaves. Slavery took many forms during that time, and while some of it was comparable to the cruel and forced slavery of colonial America, most of ancient slavery did not look that way. The Bible does not deal with the problem of slavery directly. Neither Jesus nor Paul advocated the overthrow of it. The New Testament teaching on slavery deals with the slave-master relationship. Christian slave masters are to treat their slaves with fairness. Servants are to be obedient (Col. 3:22–4:1), but if a slave could attain freedom, then they ought to—"You were bought with a price; do not become bondservants of men" (1 Cor. 7:21-23). As Christianity spread, its teaching would transform and eventually eliminate slavery in many places.

The General Structure of Philemon

1. Introduction (1:1-7)
2. Paul's Request of Philemon (1:8-21)
3. Conclusion (1:22-25)

A great lesson to learn from Philemon is the use of tact and courtesy. Paul's use of it should be studied by every Christian. Christians need to learn the fine art of tactfulness in dealing with delicate situations.

LESSON 7 EXAM

Use the exam sheet at the back of the book to complete your exam.

1. **Some suggest the Colossian church was started by**
   A. Paul.
   B. Epaphras.
   C. Timothy.
   D. Silas.

2. **The theme of Colossians is**
   A. the supremacy of Christ and practical Christian living.
   B. the church as the body of Christ.
   C. a refutation of early gnosticism threatening the church.
   D. the new covenant as superior to the old covenant.

3. **The key emphasis in Colossians is Christ as the**
   A. Creator.
   B. Redeemer.
   C. Head of the body.
   D. Sustainer.

4. **Paul prayed for the Colossians that they might be**
   A. more evangelistic.
   B. filled with the knowledge of God's will.
   C. more loving to one another.
   D. more faithful in their church attendance.

5. **One preventative safeguard against heresy, says Paul, is**
   A. a thorough knowledge of the heresy.
   B. a strong prayer life.
   C. establishment in the truth.
   D. no contact with heretics.

6. **One of the three heresies identified by Paul was**
   A. mysticism.
   B. the new age.
   C. pan-theism.
   D. evolution.

7. **Paul exhorted the Colossians to be virtuous with a determination to let the**
   A. Holy Spirit empower them.
   B. believers admonish one another.
   C. peace of God rule in their hearts.
   D. allow for speaking in tongues and prophecy.

8. **One of the two purposes of Philemon was to**
   A. ask Philemon for lodging.
   B. instruct Philemon to release all his slaves.
   C. warn Philemon of the coming apostasy.
   D. teach Philemon how to choose elders in the church.

9. **The meaning of Onesimus' name is**
   A. worthy.   C. profitable.
   B. lover of God.   D. joyous.

10. **The key expression of Philemon is**
   A. "release him."   C. "receive him."
   B. "restore him."   D. "revive him."

What Do You Say?

How has this lesson increased your knowledge of and appreciation for Christ?

LESSON 8

1 and 2 Thessalonians

THE FIRST LETTER TO THE THESSALONIANS

Background

The city of Thessalonica (modern Salonika) was located on the Thermaic Gulf. The famous Roman road known as the Egnatian Way, which spanned Macedonia, passed through the walls of Thessalonica. Because of this road, Thessalonica was in ready contact with other districts and cities which aided the city commercially. Its fine harbor was Macedonia's major outlet to the Aegean Sea giving it maritime contacts with the rest of the Mediterranean world. It is estimated by scholars that Thessalonica had a large population of about 200,000 consisting primarily of Greeks but also including Jewish people, Romans, and Asiatics.

There was a Jewish synagogue there which had been instrumental in proselytizing a considerable number of Greeks (Acts 17:4). It was an ideal place to preach the Gospel, and Paul eventually made his way there from Philippi passing through Amphipolis and Apollonia. Upon arriving in Thessalonica, as his custom was, he preached in the synagogue for three Sabbaths (Acts 17:1-9). Some Jewish people, and a great number of Greek proselytes (called "devout Greeks"), believed the Gospel and joined themselves to Paul. Persecution broke out so that the believers sent Paul, Silas, and Timothy away by night to Berea. Persecution followed them there and so Paul went on to Athens (Acts 17:13-15) and later Corinth

(Acts 18:1), leaving Silas and Timothy temporarily in Berea. It was from Corinth that Paul wrote back to the Thessalonians the two epistles being considered in this lesson.

The Author of 1 Thessalonians

According to 1:1, the apostle Paul wrote this letter and he included with him in the salutation Silvanus (Silas) and Timothy. They were with Paul in Thessalonica when the Gospel was preached and the church established.

Date, Place, and Occasion for Writing

Paul wrote 1 Thessalonians in approximately AD 50 or 51 on his second missionary journey. He came to Athens, leaving Timothy and Silas in Macedonia. Later they joined him in Athens as Paul had commanded (Acts 17:15). While in Athens, Paul was greatly concerned for the afflicted believers in Thessalonica, so he sent Timothy back to find out their situation and comfort them (3:1-6). Before Timothy returned, Paul had moved on to Corinth to evangelize. It was there Timothy met up with him (Acts 18:5), and conveyed the good news of the endurance and perseverance of the Thessalonian church (3:7-10). This good news prompted Paul to write the first of his epistles to them.

The Theme and Purpose of 1 Thessalonians

The theme of 1 Thessalonians is the Second Coming of Jesus Christ. This theme is mentioned at least once in each chapter (1:9-10; 2:17-20; 3:11-13; 4:13-18; 5:23-24). The purpose comes out of the theme. Paul wrote primarily to encourage and challenge these young believers to endurance, service, assurance, and holiness of life in the light of the sure coming of Jesus Christ.

The Personal Quality of the Letter

1 Thessalonians is much like Philippians in this regard. Paul opened his heart in speaking of the warm and tender relationship he had with them while there. He showed a sincere shepherd care in chapter three where he was intensely concerned about their welfare. Paul never once criticizes the Thessalonians!

The General Outline Structure of the Letter

1. Personal Relationship of Paul and the Thessalonians (1:1–3:13)
2. Practical Ministry and Exhortation (4:1–5:28)

The Flow of Development of 1 Thessalonians

Let's take a closer at these two sections.

1. Personal Relationship of Paul and the Thessalonians (1:1–3:13)

Paul's Thanksgiving for the Thessalonians (1:1-10)

Paul gives thanks to God for two things. First, he thanks God for the spiritual life of these new believers (1:1-3). He points out three areas of evidence for the reality of their new life: their works produced by faith, their labor produced by love, and their patience (steadfastness) produced by hope. Secondly, he thanks God for the fact that they have been chosen of Him (1:4-10). How did Paul know this? He gives three evidences to confirm his knowledge: he knew they were chosen by the way the Word of God came to them (1:4-5), by the way they had received the word (1:6), and by the impact their testimony was having in the world (1:7-10). When others view your life, do they know you are God's chosen?

> **When others view your life, do they know you are God's chosen?**

Paul's Reminder to the Thessalonians of the Nature of His Ministry While Among Them—A Model Servant (2:1-16)

It would appear from the description Paul gives of himself in this section that some had accused him of serving God from base motives. He points out to the Thessalonians that he had been an example of what a servant should be. He was courageous (2:1-2), honest (2:3-6), gentle and selfless (2:7-9), and blameless before them (2:10-12). Their response to his preaching was positive. They received the preaching of Paul as God's Word, not man's. In doing so, they suffered like other churches (2:13-16).

Paul's Concern for Their Present Welfare (2:17–3:13)

To Paul, the Thessalonians were his joy and crown. He had wanted to go back and visit them on more than one occasion but Satan, in some way, hindered him in accomplishing this (2:17-20). So he sent Timothy to find out their situation. Timothy returned with a very positive report and Paul was thrilled (3:1-13)!

2. Practical Ministry and Exhortation (4:1-5:28)

Instruction on Practical Sanctification (4:1-8)

Paul had generally taught the Thessalonians how to walk and please God, but there was still room for improvement, and so he encouraged them to excel still more (4:1-2). Specifically he calls upon them to abstain from sexual immorality (4:3-8). This is a problem in our day as much as it was in Paul's.

Exhortation to Love (4:9-12)

This is the second exhortation to brotherly love in this letter (see 3:11-13). Paul acknowledged that they were loving one another, and that they had been taught of God to love. However, there is always room for growth, and so he calls upon them to excel still more in this virtue. Love is the key ingredient for a successful unity in the body of Christ and witness to the world (John 13:34-35).

Clarification Concerning the Second Coming (4:13-18)

Some of the Thessalonians seem to have understood Paul to teach, while he was with them, that all believers would live until Christ returned. When some of their number died, the question arose as to whether they would have part in the Second Coming. Paul clarified by saying that those Christians who have died would indeed take part in Christ's coming. Here is the order:

1. Resurrection of dead Christians at Christ's coming (4:13-14, 16)
2. Rapture ("caught up") of living Christians at Christ's coming (4:17)
3. Reunion ("caught up together") to be with the Lord (4:17)
4. Reassurance—"so we will always be with the Lord" (4:17)
5. Responsibility—"Therefore encourage one another with these words" (4:18)

Teaching Concerning the Day of the Lord (5:1-11)

The term "day of the Lord" is a technical term used over and over again in the Old Testament primarily for God's great judgments in the earth after the church has been "caught up" (raptured) to heaven. The Christian church will not go through that period (Rev. 3:10). The intent of this passage is to instruct the Thessalonians (and us) that God has not appointed us for that day of coming wrath (5:9-11). Paul says more about the "day of the Lord" in 2 Thessalonians 2.

Practical Exhortation (5:12-22)

- *Exhortation of a Relational Nature (5:12-15)*—What should be one's attitude toward leaders (5:12-13)? Leaders who diligently labor among God's people should receive appreciation and esteem. What kind of ministry should one have toward people who have negative characteristics (5:14-15)? The general rule is be patient toward all and take no revenge. Specifically, the idle are to be admonished (warned), the faint-hearted are to be encouraged, and the weak are to be supported. Possibly the "weak" refer to believers who are constantly distracted and find it difficult to make moral decisions.
- *Exhortation of a Personal Nature (5:16-22)*—In the devotional life (16-18), one is to keep praying, rejoicing, and giving thanks. In the religious life (5:19-21), believers are not to hinder spiritual ministries. Rather, they should examine everything carefully and hold fast to what is good. In the moral life (5:22), Christians are to abstain from every form (appearance) of evil.

Conclusion (5:23-28)

Paul concludes with a benediction (5:23-24) in which he prays for the preservation and sanctification of the believers. He makes a request (5:25) of the brethren to pray for him and his team of missionaries. He calls on them to greet the brethren with a holy kiss (5:26). He charges them to have this letter read to all the brethren (5:27). Finally, Paul gives his favorite wish for them—God's grace (5:28).

> **Let us keep Christ's coming ever before us so that we might be comforted, challenged, and holy.**

This letter reminds all of us that Jesus is coming. His coming is viewed in relation to salvation (1:9-10), service (2:17-20), sanctification (3:11-13), solace (4:13-18), and preservation (5:23). Let us keep His coming ever before us so that we might be comforted, challenged, and holy.

THE SECOND LETTER TO THE THESSALONIANS

Background

Some of the same general background given for 1 Thessalonians applies to this letter as well—author (Paul), readers (the Thessalonian church) and dominant theme (the Second Coming of Christ).

The Purpose

Paul needed to make some clarification concerning their sufferings, give correction concerning the "day of the Lord," and give a strong charge concerning some practical matters. How did he know that these things needed to be done? It seems logical that whoever was the messenger to deliver the first epistle found out about their new difficulties after he arrived in Thessalonica to deliver 1 Thessalonians. He informed Paul about this, and therefore Paul wrote the second epistle.

Date Of Writing 2 Thessalonians

Given the nature of the difficulties discussed in 2 Thessalonians, it is not hard to conceive that Paul wrote back almost immediately. Probably there was just a month or two between the writing of the two epistles making the date the same—AD 50–51.

The General Structure of 2 Thessalonians

1. Clarification Concerning Their Sufferings (1:1-12)
2. Correction Concerning the Day of the Lord (2:1-17)
3. Challenges and Commands Concerning Practical Matters (3:1-18)

The Flow of Development of 2 Thessalonians

1. Clarification Concerning Their Sufferings (1:1-12)

Before giving clarification concerning their suffering, Paul gives his usual salutation and thanksgiving. This is practically the same as in the first letter. He is very grateful that their faith and love have grown exceedingly, and that the suffering and persecutions they have gone through have strengthened their faith rather than destroyed it (1:1-4). Compare Romans 5:3-4.

Paul is proud of the way the Thessalonians have handled their sufferings, and he spoke proudly of them among the churches for their perseverance and faith. To encourage them to keep enduring, he instructs that endurance is an evidence of God working in them, supporting them and fitting them for the kingdom (1:5). Ultimate relief will come when the Lord comes to earth in power, glory, and judgment upon His enemies. Then He will establish His kingdom (1:7-10). In the meantime, Paul prayed that they might live for God and thus be counted worthy of their calling, and in the process glorify the Lord Jesus Christ (1:11-12).

2. Correction Concerning the Day of the Lord (2:1-17)

Paul had taught the Thessalonians in his first letter (5:1-11) that the "day of the Lord" was yet future and that believers in the church age would not go through that period (1 Thess. 5:9-11). However, false teaching which contradicted Paul's instruction on this doctrine was being circulated to the effect that the "day of the Lord" had indeed come upon them. It was falsely claimed that this inaccurate teaching had come come from Paul via spirit, word (message), or letter. The Thessalonians were shaken by this and were losing their composure. Paul corrected this error by teaching that it was impossible for them to be in "the day of the Lord" for two major events had not yet occurred that signal that time period. What are these? First, "the day of the Lord" must be preceded by the apostasy (2 Thess. 2:3a). "The" apostasy is not just an unbelieving spirit among men, but an aggressive and powerful revolt against God. Secondly, the revelation of "the man of lawlessness" (the Anti-Christ) had not occurred (2:3b-12). This man cannot be revealed until the "restrainer," the Holy Spirit, ceases His restraining ministry. Therefore, the Thessalonians should be encouraged that they, in spite of their tribulations and sufferings, are not going through that awful period which is described in detail in Revelation 6–19. Paul's correction must have brought great relief and peace to their troubled minds.

> **Ultimate relief will come when the Lord comes to earth in power, glory, and judgment upon His enemies.**

3. Challenges and Commands Concerning Practical Matters (3:1-18)

Paul exhorts them to pray for him, and he is confident in their faithfulness to his instruction (3:1-5). Paul commands that they keep away from unruly and disobedient believers (3:6-15). Paul concludes by authenticating the letter with his own signature and then pronouncing the benediction of grace upon them (3:17-18).

One important lesson for believers today comes out of the correcting ministry of Paul concerning "the day of the Lord." That teaching should be a good illustration to us of how important it is to be well grounded in the truth. They lost their peace and composure through the propagation of error. Study hard. Get to know the Scriptures well so that your mind may always be at peace and your composure never lost.

LESSON 8 EXAM

Use the exam sheet at the back of the book to complete your exam.

1. **The largest people group in Thessalonica was the**
    A. Greeks.
    B. Jews.
    C. Romans.
    D. Asiatics.

2. **Paul wrote 1 and 2 Thessalonians from the city of**
    A. Berea.
    B. Athens.
    C. Corinth.
    D. Apollonia.

3. **The theme of 1 Thessalonians is the**
    A. day of the Lord.
    B. salvation of the soul.
    C. sanctification of the believer.
    D. second coming of Christ.

4. **As a servant example, Paul was**
    A. courageous.
    B. honest.
    C. gentle and selfless.
    D. all of the above.

5. **In 1 Thessalonians 4:3-8, Paul called upon the Thessalonians to abstain from**
    A. lying and stealing.
    B. the worship of idols.
    C. sexual immorality.
    D. laziness and gluttony.

6. **The term "day of the Lord"**
    A. refers primarily to God's great blessing in the earth.
    B. is synonymous with the rapture of the church to heaven.
    C. is a technical term used primarily of God's judgment in the earth.
    D. none of the above.

7. **One of Paul's purposes in writing 2 Thessalonians was to**
   A. give correction concerning "the day of the Lord."
   B. exhort to brotherly love.
   C. warn against arrogant attitudes.
   D. settle a dispute between two sisters.

8. **Paul was proud of the way the Thessalonians had handled their**
   A. friendship with the lost.
   B. economic crisis.
   C. church problems.
   D. sufferings.

9. **"The apostasy" referred to in 2 Thessalonians was**
   A. simply an unbelieving spirit among men.
   B. an aggressive and powerful revolt against God.
   C. a temporary backsliding of a believer.
   D. all of the above.

10. **What kind of person does Paul warn the Thessalonians about?**
    A. false teachers.
    B. division makers.
    C. ignorant Christians.
    D. unruly and disobedient believers.

What Do You Say?

How does the subject of the second coming of Christ and the resurrection of believers dealt with by Paul in 1 Thessalonians offer comfort to you?

---

1 Timothy, Titus, and 2 Timothy

THE FIRST LETTER TO TIMOTHY

Background

First Timothy is the first of three letters of Paul that have been traditionally called the pastoral epistles (letters). The other two are 2 Timothy and Titus. The term "pastoral epistles" means that these letters have to do with the shepherd-care ministry of individuals and local churches. These letters were named after the men to whom they were sent. This does not mean that they were clergymen in charge of the local congregations. It is clear that they were sent to churches on temporary missions by the apostle Paul to instruct believers and warn them against false teachers and teaching.

Timothy was the child of a mixed marriage. His mother was Jewish, while his father (name unknown) was Greek (Acts 16:1-3). Timothy's grandmother Lois and his mother Eunice are mentioned in 2 Timothy 1:5. Both were women of faith. There is no indication that his father was a believer. As a young boy, Timothy was well-trained in the Holy Scriptures (2 Tim. 3:15) and this was good preparation for that day when Paul preached the Gospel in his home city and Timothy was saved. Paul calls him "my true child in the faith" (1 Tim. 1:2). On the second missionary journey, Paul revisited the area where Timothy lived (Acts 16:1-3). Paul invited him to join the missionary team. He circumcised him so that his Greek ancestry would not be a problem when evangelizing among Jewish people (Acts 16:3). Timothy shared in Paul's evangelistic labors in Macedonia and Achaia (Acts 17:14–15; 18:5), and was with Paul during his lengthy preaching ministry at Ephesus (Acts 19:22). He traveled with Paul from Ephesus to Macedonia, to Corinth, back to Macedonia and to Asia Minor (Acts 20:1-6). It is possible that he traveled with Paul to Jerusalem after the third missionary journey was complete. He was with Paul during his first imprisonment (Phil. 1:1; Col. 1:1; Philem. 1:1) in Rome. Following Paul's release from this first imprisonment (Acts 28), Timothy again traveled with Paul but eventually stayed at Ephesus, at Paul's urging, to deal with problems there (1 Tim. 1:3).

> Legalism is an insult to the work of Christ upon the cross.

The Author of 1 Timothy

According to the salutation (1:1), the apostle Paul wrote this letter. Many modern critics of the Bible question Paul's authorship of the pastoral letters more than any others, but much of their opposition is based on a skeptical approach to the Bible and subjective assumptions or presuppositions. There is no evidential or objective reason to doubt Paul's authorship, or the historical accuracy of the opening verse.

The Date, Place and Occasion of Writing

Paul was in Macedonia when he wrote 1 Timothy. He had left Timothy in Ephesus to minister to some problems the church was facing. The occasion for writing was to tell Timothy that he was coming back to rejoin him, but that he was not exactly sure when this would be (3:14; 4:13). 1 Timothy was written between Paul's two Roman imprisonments. Paul was released from the first imprisonment about AD 62, and he wrote 1 Timothy somewhere between AD 63 and 65.

Paul's Purpose in Writing 1 Timothy

The content of the letter makes the purpose for writing very clear. Paul wrote to him for a threefold purpose: to encourage him in his own personal life, to instruct him on how to handle certain situations in the church, and to give counsel on such practical matters as prayer, leadership, widows, etc.

The General Structure of 1 Timothy

1. Sound Doctrine of God's Grace (1:1-20)
2. Scriptural Order of the Church (2:1–3:16)
3. Spiritual Discernment for the Last Days (4:1-11)
4. Steadfast Testimony of Timothy to the Ephesians (4:12-16)
5. Some Instructions Concerning Various Groups (5:1–6:10)
6. Concluding Matters (6:11-21)

The Flow of Development of 1 Timothy

1. Sound Doctrine of God's Grace (1:1-20)

Paul warned the church of Ephesus many years before (Acts 20:28-32) that false teachers would arise from among their own membership, and from without. That prophecy has come to pass. The nature of the false teaching was Jewish legalism which was the opposite of the sound doctrine of grace. Timothy was charged by Paul to stop the Judaizing teachers in their pursuit to mix the law with grace (1:3-4). To clarify, Paul says that the law has its place when used lawfully (1:8-11)—to convict sinners, but not to save and sanctify believers. Paul's own testimony was that it was God's grace and mercy that saved him—the chief of sinners—not the law (1:12-17). Thus Timothy is to fight the good fight of God's grace, keeping faith and a good conscience which others have rejected, causing themselves ruin (1:18-20).

The problem of legalism in the church did not die in the first century. It is still with us today! It is an insult to the work of Christ upon the cross and the sanctifying ministry of the Holy Spirit in the life of the believer.

2. Scriptural Order of the Church (2:1–3:16)

Public Prayer in the Local Church (2:1-15)

Paul called for prayer for all people, singling out kings and all who are in authority (2:1-2a). The purpose was clear: that the church might lead a tranquil and quiet life in all godliness and dignity (2:2b). Paul evaluated this as being good and acceptable to God our Savior (2:3). Prayer is good for all because God desires all to be saved (2:4). He made this possible by giving Jesus as the only mediator (2:5), and ransom for sin for all mankind (2:6). This message of the cross, says Paul, is what he was appointed to preach (2:7).

From this call for prayer in the public meetings, Paul moves on to the conduct expected in the public meetings. Men (male believers) are given the responsibility to pray in the meetings (2:8). Women are to be modestly adorned in the public meeting, to submit to instruction, and not to teach or exercise authority over the man (2:9-15).

Leadership in the Local Church (3:1-16)

The New Testament church had two categories of leaders—elders (also called overseers), and deacons. Paul gives the qualifications of elders in 3:1-7 and those of deacons in 3:8-12. The qualifications for both are practically the same, touching the areas of the spiritual, social, domestic, and moral. These qualifications should be known and understood before any steps are taken to recognize men for leadership.

You have a gift from God. Are you using it?

By way of conclusion to chapters 2 and 3, Paul says he wrote these things in order that believers would know how to behave in the church. Chapters 2 and 3 do not exhaust what the New Testament says about the church and its functions, but they do give instruction that the Ephesian church needed at the time.

3. Spiritual Discernment for the Last Days (4:1-11)

Paul taught that in later times some professing Christians would depart from faith. They would be influenced by deceitful spirits and doctrines of demons. In this context, the false doctrine consists of a false *asceticism*—abstaining from marriage and the eating of certain foods. Both marriage and eating are ordained of God (4:1-5)! Timothy is to teach a balance between the spiritual and the physical (4:6-11). Godliness is always profitable while bodily discipline (referring in the context to asceticism) is of little profit in this life only.

4. Steadfast Testimony of Timothy to the Ephesians (4:12-16)

At this juncture Timothy was exhorted to be a consistent Christian in personal and public life. In his personal life (4:12), he is exhorted to let no one despise his youth—that is, to give anyone a reason to condemn him. How can this be accomplished? By being a positive example in speech, conduct, love, faith, and purity. In other words, he has to be careful to practice what he preaches!

In his public life (4:13-16), he was to read, teach, and exhort the Scriptures. Believers did not have their own copies of the Scriptures, and so public reading would help them get to know content. Teaching would give them understanding, and exhorting would challenge the believers to obey. Paul says that if he does these things he will ensure that he will not neglect the gift God gave him. You have a gift from God. Are you using it?

5. Some Instructions Concerning Various Groups (5:1-6:10)

General—The Elderly and the Young (5:1-2)

Timothy was instructed on how to treat fellow believers of every age group and sex. He is to treat them as he would his own family–with respect, humility, and purity. Not to do so would ruin the influence and the effectiveness of his ministry.

Specific—Four Groups Are Emphasized (5:3–6:10)

These four groups are widows (5:3-16), elders (5:17-25), slaves (6:1-2), and false teachers (6:3-10). Widowhood, though a difficult problem today, was a great crisis in ancient days. There were some who desperately needed the help of the church. Paul gives instruction on how to determine a widow who is eligible for support. Elders that work hard at teaching and preaching are worthy of double honor—both respect and financial assistance. Slaves are to be obedient and respectful toward their masters— especially to those masters who are believers. Finally, Paul describes the moral and spiritual condition of false teachers (those who advocate teaching contrary to sound doctrine). These, he says, look upon religion as a means of making gain. On the contrary, says Paul, "godliness with contentment is great gain" (6:6)!

6. Concluding Matters (6:11-21)

Paul brings this first letter to Timothy to a close by exhorting Timothy to have a powerful life for God (6:11-16), and to warn rich believers to use their wealth for God (6:17-19). Lastly he charges Timothy to guard what has been entrusted to him—the Gospel. Don't let it get mixed with error!

THE LETTER TO TITUS

Background

In our Bibles, the letter to Titus follows 2 Timothy. Chronologically, however, it comes before 2 Timothy which is the last letter Paul wrote. We will survey it before 2 Timothy.

Paul wrote this letter while Titus was on the Island of Crete. Crete is the fourth largest island in the Mediterranean. It is located due south of the Aegean Sea. The apostle Paul visited Crete as a prisoner on his voyage to Rome (Acts 27). The island of Crete is about 155 miles long and ranges from 6 to 35 miles wide. It is mainly mountainous. The inhabitants of Crete, as witnessed by some ancient historians (Livy, Plutarch, Polybius, Strabo), had a very evil reputation. Two popular expressions quoted about the Cretans were very unflattering. "To Cretize" meant to lie, and "to play the Cretan with a Cretan" meant to out-trick a trickster. Paul describes the Cretans in Titus 1:12 as "always liars, evil beasts, lazy gluttons." Paul says, "this testimony is true" (1:13). Paul's source for this description was one of the Cretan's own writers, Epimenides. Epimenides is also quoted by Paul in Acts 17:28a. Thus you can perceive that Titus' mission in Crete was going to be very difficult.

The Author of Titus

The salutation tells us that the apostle Paul is the author. He describes himself as both a servant and an apostle. The word servant relates Paul to God who is his Master. The word apostle relates Paul to the church. The one is a vertical relationship and the other a horizontal relationship. The one emphasizes his submission to God's Lordship over his life and the other emphasizes the use of his gift of apostleship for the good of God's people.

The Recipient of the Epistle—Titus

There is no mention of Titus in the book of Acts. We have to draw our materials for a biographical sketch of Titus from other New Testament books. He was a convert of Paul (1:4). He is mentioned 13 times in Paul's letters. Nine of these are found in 2 Corinthians. He was a Greek (Gal. 3:2). As a Greek convert to Jesus, Titus became a test case (Gal. 2:1-3) for

Gentile admission to the church solely on the basis of faith. He was a very trusted associate of Paul as seen by the task Paul gave him of collecting the gift for the poor saints in Jerusalem (2 Cor. 8–9). His trustworthiness is also seen by the fact that Paul left Titus in Crete as his representative to establish the churches there (Titus 1:5). Paul and Titus had gone to Crete some time after Paul was released from his first Roman imprisonment. They evangelized and many were saved in the various cities. Paul had to leave, but left Titus to continue the work of establishing the new converts in the Lord and appointing elders in every city (1:5). The general picture we get of Titus is that he was an energetic, vigorous and forceful man of God. He was one who could work with and for another. He was loyal and responsible. We need many like him in the church of Jesus Christ today!

> **Paul believed in good works, not to obtain salvation but as tangible evidence of the genuineness of a person's salvation.**

The Date, Place and Occasion of Writing

The occasion of writing was Paul's summons for Titus to return (3:12-14). Paul was sending either Artemas or Tychicus to Crete. When one or the other arrived, Titus was to make every effort to return and meet Paul in Nicopolis where he had planned to spend the winter. We have no knowledge if this came about, but we do know that Titus was in Rome for some of the time during Paul's second imprisonment there (see 2 Tim. 4:10). Paul may have been in Macedonia when he wrote to Titus. We know he was there when he wrote 1 Timothy. The date of writing Titus would be the same as 1 Timothy—about AD 63–65.

The Purpose of Writing Titus

The content of Titus makes it clear that Paul's primary purpose in writing this epistle was to give Titus counsel and commands regarding his ministry in Crete. Paul knew exactly what was needed and gave explicit instructions on what actions Titus should take and what ministry he should give.

A Key Expression in Titus—"Good Works"

Paul believed in good works, not to obtain salvation but as tangible evidence of the genuineness of a person's profession of salvation. There are six references to good works in Titus (1:16; 2:7, 14; 3:1, 8, 14). Paul makes it clear in 2:14 and 3:8 that good works come after a person is saved.

Two Key Passages of Titus

Titus 2:11-14 deals with God's grace as related to salvation, sanctification, and glorification. God's grace appeared in the past bringing salvation to all (2:11, 14). The grace of God presently teaches us to live moral and spiritual lives (2:12). Finally, God's grace points to the future, to the blessed hope of the second appearing of our Savior.

Titus 3:4-7 teaches us that the salvation which God's grace brought through Jesus Christ is not realized by our own works of righteousness but by His mercy.

The General Structure of Titus

1. Instruction Concerning Church Leaders (1:1-9)
2. Instruction Concerning False Teachers (1:10-16)
3. Instruction Concerning The Christian Household (2:1-15)
4. Instruction Concerning Various Responsibilities (3:1-15)

The Flow of Development of Titus

1. Instruction Concerning Church Leaders (1:1-9)

For a church to function properly and successfully there must be leadership—but not just any kind of leadership. Given the kind of culture-characteristics of the Cretan, there would be the need of strong leaders. Paul, as he did in 1 Timothy 3, gives the qualifications that church leaders in Crete would need to raise strong and established churches.

2. Instruction Concerning False Teachers (1:10-16)

Ungodly and rebellious men, especially from the circumcision, were causing chaos among believing families by their wicked teachings. Their motivation was material gain (compare 1 Tim. 6:3-10). Paul commands Titus to silence them and severely rebuke them. They profess that they know God but in works they deny Him. This is a problem that still exists in the modern church. Godly leaders today have to be just as strong and severe as Titus was in order to preserve the church from destruction.

3. Instruction Concerning the Christian Household (2:1-15)

Paul calls upon all the groups of a household (the old, the young, men, women, and slaves) to adorn the doctrine of God by godly conduct. The incentives to this are God's grace in salvation (2:11-12), the coming of Jesus (2:13), and Christ's purpose in redeeming us—"purify for Himself a people for His own possession who are zealous for good works" (2:14).

4. Instruction Concerning Various Responsibilities (3:1-15)

First, Paul charges believers to be subject to civil authorities (3:1-7). This is one way that these former rebels (3:3) can demonstrate the transforming power of the Gospel in their lives (3:4-7). Secondly, in the church they are to be known for good works (3:8), avoid religious controversy (3:9), and reject factious persons from fellowship after two warnings (3:10-11).

THE SECOND LETTER TO TIMOTHY

Background

This is the last of Paul's letters, written from a dungeon in Rome according to tradition. Paul had experienced a previous imprisonment in Rome a few years earlier. At that time he wrote the prison letters. Let us observe the major differences between the two imprisonments:

FIRST IMPRISONMENT	SECOND IMPRISONMENT
Christianity was legal	Christianity was illegal (declared by the Roman Emperor, Nero)
Paul given much liberty	Confined as a criminal against the state (2 Tim. 2:9)
Accessible to all (Acts 28:30)	Difficult to find (2 Tim. 2:9)
Confined in a hired house (Acts 28)	Roman dungeon (tradition)
Surrounded by a considerable number of co-workers (Col. 4:10-14; Phil. 1:13-14)	Almost alone. Many had left him and only Luke was with him (2 Tim. 4:9-11)

He expected release (Phil. 1:25-26; 2:24)	He looked forward to death (2 Tim. 4:6)
He expected further labors for Christ upon his release (Phil. 1:21-26)	He expected the crown of righteousness for a faithful life of service (2 Tim. 4:7-8)

In both imprisonments, Paul's spirit was strong and his love was abundant toward others. However, there must have been great sorrow in his heart as he thought of those who had forsaken him and the Gospel they once professed to love.

The Author

The salutation identifies the author as the apostle Paul. He reminds Timothy that his apostleship was "by the will of God." God had told Ananias (Acts 9:14) that Paul's service as an apostle would mean much suffering. Paul, as he writes this letter, is about to suffer the ultimate for his service—death (4:6). He has been faithful from first to last!

The Recipient—Timothy

Timothy was probably still in Ephesus fulfilling his pastoral assignment (as urged by Paul, 1 Tim. 1:3) when Paul wrote to him. He wished for Timothy (1:1-2) what he would desperately need in a world that outlawed Christianity: grace, mercy, and peace!

The Place and Date of Writing 2 Timothy

Clearly, Paul was in Rome, in prison, when he wrote to Timothy (1:17). The date of writing was between AD 64 (when Nero declared Christianity an illegal religion) and AD 67. Paul was probably arrested shortly after that and taken to Rome for trial (4:14-18). He may have been in Troas at the time of the arrest, since he asked Timothy to stop there on his way to Rome and get some of his belongings.

The Purpose for Writing 2 Timothy

It only takes one reading of 2 Timothy to see that it is a highly personal and practical letter to Paul's younger and beloved associate. The book is filled with exhortations to Timothy which tells us that one of Paul's major purposes was to encourage this young man in his personal life and ministry

(1:6, 8, 13-14; 2:2, 14-15, 22; 3:14; 4:2, 5). Another purpose was to instruct Timothy to come to Paul in Rome (4:9, 11, 13). A third was to acquaint Timothy with his success at his first defense (4:14-17), and to communicate his prospects for the future—death, heaven, and reward (4:6-8, 18).

Some Points of Interest

People—there are no fewer than 23 people mentioned in this brief book. Some of these are approved (like Timothy, Lois, Eunice, Onesiphorus), some are sorrowed over (like Phygellus and Hermogenes), and some are condemned (Alexander the coppersmith).

The classic statement on the inspiration of Scripture is given in 2 Timothy 3:16. *Inspiration* means "God-breathed." The Bible has its origin in God. Trust it!

The General Structure of 2 Timothy

1. The Charge to Be Unashamed in His Testimony (1:1-18)
2. The Charge to Be Strong in His Service for Christ (2:1-26)
3. The Charge to Stand Firm in the Faith in the Face of the Coming Apostasy (3:1–4:8)
4. The Conclusion (4:9-22)

The Flow of Development of 2 Timothy

1. The Charge to Be Unashamed in His Testimony (1:1-18)

What caused Timothy to be ashamed? It was fear (1:7). Fear of what? Fear of imprisonment, or of losing his life? Why was that a possibility? Because Nero had outlawed Christianity, and Paul was already suffering imprisonment and impending death due to that decree. But there is no need for fear and shame. Why? Because "God gave us a spirit not of fear but of power and love and self-control" (1:7). As well, the future is secure for us no matter what may happen, for our God has "abolished death and brought life and immortality to light through the Gospel" (1:10). Also, Paul says, God "is able to guard until that day what has been entrusted to me" (1:12). Though many were ashamed and had turned away from Paul (1:15), there were those who had not, such as Onesiphorus (1:16-18). Timothy should be like him.

2. The Charge to Be Strong in His Service for Christ (2:1-26)

In this section, Paul pictures the Christian life under seven metaphors. These metaphors describe the Christian life from seven different perspectives.

- *The Child Metaphor (2:1-2).* This metaphor pictures the Christian life as dependent on God. A child is not known for their strength. They need the support of others. So Timothy, as a child of God, needs God's grace to accomplish his ministry. We do, too!
- *The Soldier Metaphor (2:3-4).* This metaphor pictures the Christian life as a warfare (compare Ephesians 6:10-20). The emphasis is on enduring hardship and being separated from the entanglements of the world. Does the world have a stranglehold on you?
- *The Athletic Metaphor (2:5).* This metaphor pictures the Christian life as an athletic contest. To win the prize, one has to play by the rules. God's rules for the Christian race are the Bible, so the believer needs to know it thoroughly!
- *The Farmer Metaphor (2:6-13).* This metaphor pictures the Christian life as a hard-working farmer. The farmer that works hard will have a successful crop and be the first to partake of it. The Christian who labors hard sowing the seed of God's Word can expect a reward for his labor. After giving this metaphor, Paul asked Timothy (and us) to think about what he has just communicated in the first four metaphors. If he does, then the Lord will give him understanding in all things.

> The destiny of true believers is honor, but for the unbeliever, dishonor.

- *The Workman Metaphor (2:14-19).* This metaphor likens the Christian life to a person who works diligently at their profession in the everyday world. The believer must work hard at "rightly handling the word of truth" (accurately interpreting the Word).
- *The Utensil Metaphor (2:20-23).* In this metaphor, the Christian life is likened to gold and silver utensils (in contrast to wood and earthenware ones) found in a great house. The gold and silver utensils are true believers (like Timothy, Paul, Titus, etc.) whereas the wood and earthenware ones stand for professing Christians who are not true believers—like Hymenaeus and Philetus (2:17). The destiny of true believers is honor, but for the unbeliever, dishonor.

- *The Bondslave Metaphor (2:24-26).* The Christian life is likened to the service of a bondslave. The bondslave had no personal rights. They were a person in total submission to their master. The believer, like the bondslave, is in total submission to the Lord, their Master, and is to show this submission by humility, gentleness, patience, and helpfulness.

3. The Charge to Stand Firm in the Faith in the Face of the Coming Apostasy (3:1–4:8)

Toward the end of the church age ("last days") there would be great apostasy (departure) from the faith. Professed believers would be characterized by a self-centered and arrogant life-style (3:1-4); their religion would be merely external, lacking the Holy Spirit (3:5a); they are to be avoided (3:5b); their evil fruits consist of gross immorality and a false intellectualism (3:6-9). Timothy, says Paul, has not fallen prey to these deceivers. Rather, he has followed the apostolic doctrine and example (3:10-13). The power against apostasy and apostates is the Word of God (3:14–4:8). Timothy has known that Word since childhood and Paul reminds him that it is inspired of God and profitable to mature and equip him for every good work. If all this about the Word is so (and it is!), then Timothy should preach the Word (4:1-5)—especially in light of the fact that Paul would soon be departing for heaven (4:6-8).

4. The Conclusion (4:9-22)

In the conclusion, Paul charged Timothy to come to Rome and bring Mark with him, along with some of Paul's possessions which he had left at Troas. He closes with some information (good and bad) on mutual friends, speaks of his situation, and gives greetings and a benediction.

LESSON 9 EXAM

Use the exam sheet at the back of the book to complete your exam.

1. **Timothy came from a family where**
   A. his parents were both Jewish.
   B. his parents were both Gentiles.
   C. his mother was Jewish and his father a Greek.
   D. his father was Jewish and his mother a Roman.

2. **In 1 Timothy 1:1-20, Paul emphasizes the doctrine of**
   A. the Holy Spirit.   C. God's grace.
   B. holiness.   D. the Scriptures.

3. **Paul's instruction in 1 Timothy 2:1–3:16 concerns the**
   A. temple.   C. synagogue.
   B. local church.   D. home.

4. **Paul gives instructions in 1 Timothy chapters 5 and 6 concerning**
   A. older men and women.
   B. widows.
   C. elders and masters.
   D. all of the above.

5. **Paul's primary purpose in writing to Titus was to**
   A. encourage him to not give up the faith.
   B. warn him of a planned persecution against him.
   C. exhort him read the Scriptures publicly.
   D. give him counsel and commands regarding his ministry.

6. **A key expression in Titus which is mentioned six times is**
   A. "sound doctrine."
   B. "sincere conscience."
   C. "justification by faith."
   D. "good works."

7. **Titus 2:11-14 deals with God's grace as related to**
   A. good works and morality.
   B. redemption and separation.
   C. salvation, sanctification, and glorification.
   D. false teachers and fellowship.

8. **At the time Paul wrote 2 Timothy, Christianity was**
   A. illegal.
   B. well received by Jewish leaders.
   C. welcomed by the Roman empire.
   D. none of the above.

9. **The classic statement on what major doctrine of the Bible is given in 2 Timothy 3:16?**
   A. salvation by grace through faith.
   B. the inspiration of the Scriptures.
   C. spiritual liberation by the Holy Spirit.
   D. the full deity of Jesus Christ.

10. **Paul pictured the Christian as a**
   A. tent maker.   C. athlete.
   B. king.   D. sailor.

What Do You Say?

What responsibilities do you have in your local church? What is your attitude toward those responsibilities?

LESSON 10

Hebrews, James, and 1 Peter

Few people choose to suffer. Self-preservation is so instinctive in humans that we take great measures to protect ourselves and avoid suffering. But suffering comes and we cannot, with all our ingenuity, escape all of it. Suffering began with our first parents, Adam and Eve (Gen. 3) and, for the believer, it will remain until we are in heaven (Rev. 21:4). The unbeliever will suffer eternally (Rev. 20:11-15; Matt. 25:41, 46). The reasons for suffering in this life are many. A more prominent one is persecution for one's faith in Jesus Christ. Believers throughout the past 2,000 years of church history have been persecuted for their faith in the Lord Jesus Christ, ranging in extent from nasty words and ridicule to torturous deaths. The first century church suffered greatly (Acts 4, 5, 7, 12, etc.). Therefore, it is not strange that we should have books in our New Testament which deal with that problem. The three books under consideration were written to suffering believers to aid them in properly handling their affliction for Christ. Not all of the suffering mentioned in these books came as a result of persecution (compare James 1), but much of it did.

THE LETTER TO THE HEBREWS

The Author of Hebrews

The author of this wonderful letter does not give his name. Many take it for granted that Paul wrote it. Scholars are divided over the exact identity. Apollos, Barnabas, and Luke are just three of several viewed as authors.

We should keep in mind that Hebrews is the inspired Word of God and our lack of knowledge of the specific author does not hinder our understanding of it, or make it any less God's Word.

The Recipients of Hebrews

The content of the book makes it clear that the recipients of this letter were Jewish Christians. But did Hebrews have a specific destination—a specific Jewish audience in mind? Scholars are divided on this issue, too, since it has no salutation showing destination. Two notable views are Jerusalem and Rome. Coming up with a particular view is quite involved and outside the scope of a survey. This author, however, favors the view that Hebrews was written to the Jewish community in Palestine.

The Date of Writing Hebrews

Hebrews had to be written before AD 70 since the Jewish temple was still standing and being used (compare Hebrews 10:11 where the present tense for priestly ministry is used). AD 64–70 were years of great persecution for believers. A date somewhere between these years would fit the content of the book well. In Palestine from AD 66–70, the Roman-Jewish war (given in detail by the Jewish historian Josephus) was raging. One could easily understand the persecution of Jewish believers who were unwilling to take sides in the war since Jesus had predicted the destruction of Jerusalem. Some of the Jewish Christians may have been intimidated by their unsaved Jewish brethren and have found it easier to leave Christianity to go back to Judaism, and thus preserve themselves from suffering.

The Purpose of Hebrews

The major purpose of Hebrews was to show the superiority of Jesus Christ in His person and work to the Old Testament system. If He is superior—and He is—then why would any Jewish Christian want to go back to an inferior covenant of the law? Thus, Jewish Christian must go on in their New Covenant faith, exercising faith, hope, and endurance (10:32–12:29). Hebrews 12:1-2 puts it challengingly: "let us run with endurance the race that is set before us, looking to Jesus, the founder and perfecter of our faith, who for the joy that was set before Him endured the cross, despising the shame, and is seated at the right hand of the throne of God."

Some Points of Interest

Key Word of the Letter—"Better"

Hebrews is the letter of better things. The word "better" is found several times to demonstrate the superiority of the Christian's position in Christ (1:4; 6:9; 7:7, 19, 22; 8:6; 9:23; 10:34; 11:16, 35, 40).

The Warning Passages

There are several warning passages interspersed throughout the letter as the author developed his theme of the superiority of Christ to Judaism. Each of these passages is marked by the word "lest" which is used seven times (2:1; 3:12-13; 4:1, 11; 11:28; 12:3, 15-16). By interspersing them throughout the letter, the author constantly keeps before his readers the application of truth he is expounding to their present situation. This is what good preachers do. They make their point and then apply it to the congregation. Leaving all the applications to the end might cause the truth expounded to lose its practical power in their trials.

The Term "Let Us ..."

The author has several commands throughout the letter of a practical nature which begin with the exhorting words "let us." The fact that he used "us" shows that he needed the commands as well as they. There are 13 of these "let us" exhortations (4:1, 11, 14, 16; 6:1; 10:22, 23, 24; 12:1 (twice), 28; 13:13, 15). Twelve of the thirteen are positive. The first one in 12:1 is negative. The one common denominator is living out the faith. How? It is to be done with fear, diligence, confidence, sincerity, perseverance, grace, separation, and worship.

> **Living out the faith is to be done with fear, diligence, confidence, sincerity, perseverance, grace, separation, and worship.**

The General Structure of Hebrews

1. The Superiority of Jesus Christ to Judaism (1:1–10:18)
2. Practical Applications in the Light of Christ's Superiority over Judaism (10:19–13:21)

The Flow of Development of Hebrews

1. The Superiority of Jesus Christ to Judaism (1:1-10:18)

Jesus Christ Is Superior to the Prophets (1:1-3).

God spoke in Old Testament days to the fathers by the prophets, but the highest revelation came when God spoke by His Son.

Jesus Christ Is Superior to Angels (1:4–2:18).

The Old Testament shows the wonderful ministry that angelic beings had in serving God and God's people. But Jesus Christ is far superior to these created beings for He has "a better name" (1:4-14), and a "better inheritance" (2:5-18).

Jesus Christ Is Superior to Joshua and Moses (3:1–4:13).

Two of the greatest servants of God in the Old Testament were Moses and Joshua. Moses, under God, delivered Israel from Egyptian bondage and led Israel through the 40 years of wilderness wanderings. Joshua, after Moses' death, led Israel into the promised land and guided the nation in the taking of Canaan, the land of promise, the land of rest. But Jesus Christ is far superior to Moses for He was the builder (creator) of the house of Israel, whereas Moses was just a servant in it. And Joshua's promise-land rest pales before the rest into which our Lord Jesus Christ will ultimately bring His people. Bible students are not all agreed on the identification of the rest. Some view it as heaven, and others as the millennial kingdom.

Jesus Christ Is Superior to Aaron and the Levitical Priesthood (4:14–10:18)

- *Introduction (4:14–5:10).* The author begins this section with a devotional challenge (4:14-16) in view of Christ's superior high priesthood. These afflicted Jewish believers to whom he is writing are exhorted to come to the "throne of grace" so that they, in their affliction, may "obtain mercy and find grace to help in time of need." Then, in verses 1-10, he gives the two qualifications for Jesus to be high priest: first, He must be human (5:1-3, 7-9), and second, He must be called (5:4-6, 10). Jesus fulfilled both of these requirements.
- *Arguments for the Superior Priesthood of Christ (5:11–10:18).* The introduction is followed by a warning passage (5:11–6:20). Then the author gives three lines of argument to show Christ's superiority

over Aaron and the Old Testament priesthood (7:1–10:18). First, Jesus Christ is superior because He is of a superior order of priesthood—the order of Melchizedec (7:1-28). Secondly, He is superior because as a priest He ministers a better covenant in a better place. It is the new covenant and the place is heaven (8:1-13). Thirdly, He is superior because as a priest He offers a better sacrifice—Himself (9:1–10:18). His sacrifice cleanses totally from sin (9:12-14), is once for all (9:24-26), and is complete (10:11-12).

2. Practical Applications in the Light of Christ's Superiority over Judaism (10:19-13:21)

The author exhorts the believers on the basis of their access to God through the blood of Jesus to draw near with confidence to God. They should hold fast the confession of their hope without wavering (10:19-31), and remember in the process of affliction that confident endurance has great reward (10:32-39). Endurance in faith and hope has long been the proof of a person in right relationship with God. So the author gives many examples of Old Testament believers who lived by faith and endured when times were difficult (11:1-40). Believers need to stay in the Christian race (12:1-2), keeping their eyes on Jesus who suffered so greatly for them. None of them have had to die for Christ (12:4), and what sufferings they have experienced should be looked upon as the discipline of a wise heavenly Father (12:5-11). So they should not give up, but seek to live holy lives (12:12-24). Hebrews closes with various practical exhortations to Christian duties socially, personally, and religiously (13:1-21).

THE LETTER OF JAMES

The Author of James

There are four men by this name in the New Testament: James, the father of Judas (Luke 6:16); James, the son of Zebedee (Matt. 10:3-4); James, the son of Alphaeus (James the less, Mark 15:40); and James, the Lord's brother (Gal. 2:9). There is nothing in this letter which identifies which one of the four wrote it. The traditional view is that it was written by James, the Lord's brother. On what is this view based? It is based on the idea that the Lord's brother is the only James who appears to have sufficiently played a prominent part in early Christian history. It could not be the apostle James for he was martyred earlier (Acts 12:1-2). As in other cases, not knowing for certain which James wrote this letter does not hinder our understanding and appreciation for it. Actually, the most important thing we can know about the author is what he says of himself in 1:1—He was a "servant of God and of the Lord Jesus Christ."

The Date of Writing James

Scholars believe that James was written around AD 45. If this is correct, that would make James the earliest written of the New Testament books.

The Recipients of the Letter of James

According to 1:1, the letter was sent to "the twelve tribes in the Dispersion." From this we conclude that it was not sent to any particular church, but to Jewish Christians (note "my brethren" in verse 2) spread around the Mediterranean world. Their spiritual condition seemed to be quite low as witnessed by the kinds of exhortative calls to live the life of faith and holiness.

The Purpose of the Letter of James

James is an exceedingly practical book which calls for a faith that is genuine. A person with a genuine faith will learn to behave themselves as a believer by obeying God's Word.

Some Points of Interest

First, there is little trace of church organization. Elders and teachers are mentioned, but not in connection with ruling or imparting knowledge.

> James is an exceedingly practical book which calls for a faith that is genuine.

Secondly, in places, James is very much like some of the Old Testament prophets—especially Amos (compare some of James' severe remarks in chapters 4 and 5).

Thirdly, the teaching of James and our Lord's instruction in the Sermon on the Mount (Matt. 5–7) are quite similar in ethical and moral practicality.

The General Structure of James

1. Proper Perspective on the Trials of Life (1:1-27)
2. Practicing Love And Faith (2:1-18)
3. Power of the Tongue (3:1-13)
4. Portrait of Wisdom—False and True (3:14-18)
5. Problem of Materialism (4:1–5:6)
6. Practical Exhortations (5:7-20)

The Flow of Development of James

1. Proper Perspective on the Trials of Life (1:1-27)

Trials are a fact of life and the believer's attitude when they come should be one of joy. Why? Because trials are beneficial to a believer's maturity in faith, and there is the reward of the crown of life for those who endure testing (1:1-12). But we are not to confuse testings which God allows in our lives with the temptation to sin (1:13-15). The latter come, not from God, but from our own lustful hearts. Make no mistake about it, God sends only good gifts (1:16-18)! The tested believer (and no believer is without testing) must know the importance of the Word of God in his life (1:19-27). He is to "hear" the Word, which implies a teachable spirit (1:19-20); he is to "receive" the Word, which means to have the attitude of welcoming what God says, not just knowing it (1:21); and he is to practice the Word, for this is the ultimate goal of all Biblical knowledge (1:22-27).

> **Genuine faith shows its reality, not in mere words, but in works.**

2. Practicing Love and Faith (2:1-18)

It is one thing to say we are Christians and quite another to prove it by our lives. Genuine love will not show partiality. Impartiality and favoritism are incompatible (2:1-13). Genuine faith (2:14-26) shows its reality, not in mere words, but in works. James used Abraham and Rahab as illustrations of believers who showed the reality of their justification before God by their works. It was not works which justified them (Rom. 5:1-2), but their works were evidence of their justification by faith. A faith which has no accompanying works is dead.

3. Power of the Tongue (3:1-13)

Though the tongue is a very small member of one's body, it can cause great destruction. Not to sin in speech shows great maturity. To what extent? To such an extent that it sanctifies our whole personality. What should be our goal in regard to our speech? It should be to bring it totally under control. Is this one of your goals?

4. Portrait of Wisdom—False and True (3:14-18)

False wisdom (3:14-16) is evidenced by jealousy and selfish ambition (3:14). Its distinctive traits (3:15) are earthy, natural, and demonic. Its destructive consequences (3:16) are disorder and every evil thing. In our chaotic world, one does not have to look very far to observe these.

The true wisdom (3:17-18) is "from above." It comes from the fount of all wisdom, God. And thus it is pure, peaceable, gentle, reasonable, full of mercy, and good fruits, unwavering and without hypocrisy. It is interesting to observe that these traits are qualities which are embodied in Christ. When believers manifest these qualities they show themselves to be true followers of God.

5 Problem of Materialism (4:1-5:6)

There is nothing wrong with having wealth. The balance of Scripture is that if you do not have it, do not lust for it. If you do have it, then use it for God (see 1 Tim. 6:10-17). Greed is a big problem in the world and is not foreign to the church (4:1-5). The heartaches which materialism brings among God's people may be solved by the humility which comes from God's grace (4:6), and a commitment to a sanctified life (4:7-12). The balance in handling the problem of materialism is to consider God and His will in everything we do (4:13-17). Great judgment is coming upon those who misuse wealth by hoarding, withholding, abusing, and condemning of the righteous (5:1-6).

6. Practical Exhortations (5:7-20)

Believers are challenged to keep on enduring in the face of suffering (5:7-11). They are encouraged not to lose their composure and give way to swearing (5:12). Finally, they are to be engaged in the practical ministry of prayer (5:13-18), and be involved in helping to restore the fallen (5:19-20).

THE FIRST LETTER OF PETER

The Author

The Apostle Peter is said to be the author of this letter. Later Peter describes himself as "fellow elder and a witness of the sufferings of Christ, as well as a partaker in the glory that is going to be revealed."

The Readers

Peter wrote "to those who are elect exiles of the Dispersion in Pontus, Galatia, Cappadocia, Asia, and Bithynia." These were provinces located in what we know today as the country of Turkey. No specific locations are mentioned in 1 Peter and it is uncertain whether Peter was addressing Jewish Christians only, Gentile Christians only, or a combination of both. Those who believe that Peter has only Jewish believers in mind base their view on the phrase "exiles of the Dispersion …" This is taken to refer to Jewish people who were scattered throughout the Mediterranean world due to the dispersion.

The Place of Writing

First Peter 5:13 identifies the place of writing as Babylon. There is some uncertainty as to the meaning of this name. Some take it as literal Babylon. Others as a cryptogram for Rome. Not knowing for certain the place of writing does not spoil our understanding of the epistle.

The Date and Purpose of 1 Peter

Peter wrote his first letter somewhere between AD 63–65. Christianity was made an illegal religion by Nero in AD 64 and some feel that Peter wrote this letter to believers in the specific areas mentioned in 1:1-2, for the purpose of bringing them comfort, encouragement, and instruction in their sufferings. Others believe the letter was written just before the Neronic persecutions, because the passage on submitting to human government (2:13-17) is too conciliatory to have been written after the persecutions had begun. Whatever the exact date, there is no doubt that Peter's readers were suffering for their Christian life and testimony and needed encouragement not to give up the faith. I have a special place in my heart for Peter's first epistle because it was a great encouragement to me as a new Christian serving in the military to be strong in my faith in the face of persecution. When Peter talked about suffering to his readers he was not speaking from theory. He had much firsthand experience of being persecuted. One should read Acts 4–12 for a verification of this. It is interesting to see the close parallel between Acts and 1 Peter.

The General Structure of 1 Peter

1. Salutation (1:1-2)
2. Salvation and Suffering (1:3-12)
3. Sanctification and Suffering (1:13–4:19)
4. Conclusion (5:1-14)

The Flow of Development of 1 Peter

1. Salutation (1:1-2)

Peter described his readers as "elect exiles of the Dispersion in Pontus, Galatia, Cappadocia, Asia, and Bithynia, according to the foreknowledge of God the Father, in the sanctification of the Spirit, for obedience to Jesus Christ and for sprinkling with his blood." This description demonstrates that the three persons of the Holy Trinity are involved in the salvation of these believers. The Father elected (chose) them, the Holy Spirit's sanctifying ministry brought conviction of sin, righteousness, and judgment (see John 16:8-11) and the Lord Jesus Christ shed His blood for the cleansing of the soul from sin. Salvation is not automatic, however. There must be the obedience of faith.

2. Salvation and Suffering (1:3-12)

The preaching of the Gospel of free salvation through Jesus Christ was one of Peter's favorite themes. Acts 1–12 give the record of Peter's dynamic preaching (see Acts 4:12). We are not surprised to see that theme here. Peter's intent is to view the sufferings of his readers in the light of God's great salvation. The motivation for salvation is the Father's abundant mercy (1:3a), the nature of salvation is a living hope based on Christ's resurrection (1:3b), the ultimate goal of salvation is a wonderful future inheritance in heaven for every believer (1:4-5), the attitude toward salvation is great rejoicing even though they are presently suffering (1:6-9). The salvation which Peter preached was not a new message. It had its roots in the Old Testament prophets (1:10-12). Peter's general comments on salvation were intended to get his readers to view their sufferings in the broader context of God's great salvation. The testing of their faith in the midst of suffering would lead to "praise and glory and honor at the revelation of Jesus Christ" (1:7).

3. Sanctification and Suffering (1:13–4:19)

The Christian life is such that it is possible to suffer greatly in this life and still maintain a sanctified (holy) life which brings honor and glory to God. Peter exhorted the believers to whom he was ministering to live sanctified lives in the process of their sufferings. He makes the following points which are as relevant today as they were when he first wrote them.

> **Our responsibility, is to have a fervent and sincere love for each member in the family of God.**

Sanctification Toward God (1:13-21)

This sanctification requires an alert mental focus (1:13), moral (holy) behavior (1:14-16) and a serious reverence for God (1:17-21). It is foundational to all that is to follow. Without it the rest of the book would have little impact on the readers or us.

Sanctification Toward Our Brothers and Sisters in Christ (1:22–2:10)

We are all in the family of God by the new birth. Our responsibility, then, is to have a fervent and sincere love for each family member (1:22-25). This will involve putting sin out of our lives, for it causes disharmony and stunts growth (2:1); but it will also mean being committed to growth (2:2-3). To motivate the believers to such sanctified living, Peter brings before them the great position and blessings they have as members of Christ's church (2:4-10).

Sanctification Toward the World (2:11–4:19)

First, Peter exhorts that believers are to "abstain from the passions of the flesh, which wage war against your soul" (2:11-12). These "lusts" refer to evil desires of any kind. This is for the purpose of having a good testimony in the world.

Secondly, believers are to be submissive (2:13–3:12). The particular areas of submission are to the governing authorities (2:13-17), to slave masters (2:18-25), and Christian wives to their "own husbands" (3:1-7). The submissive believer will not only have a positive impact on those around him or her (2:15; 3:1-2), but will find God's commendation in the process (2:20). It is very important that, in the process of being on display before the gaze of the world, believers treat one another with great love (3:8-12; compare John 13:34-35).

Thirdly, Peter gives instruction on how believers should handle themselves in the face of persecution—that is, suffering for the sake of righteous living and testimony (3:13–4:19). They should always be ready to defend the faith (3:15-16), keeping in mind that it is better to suffer for doing good than evil (3:17). This was the example of Christ (3:18-22) who died the just for the unjust. Believers are to have the same attitude which Christ had when suffering (4:1-6), and continue to serve Him for the glory of God (4:7-11), rejoicing in their trials knowing that "you may also rejoice and be glad when His glory is revealed" (4:12-19).

4. The Conclusion to 1 Peter (5:1-14)

Peter concluded this first letter by exhorting various members of the church. He exhorts the elders of the church to be responsible in shepherding the flock of God. They are to do it in the right spirit and with the right motive. A reward awaits elders who serve faithfully (5:1-4).

The young (5:5a) are exhorted to be submissive to their elders. Then all of the believers are addressed (5:6-11). Peter makes an appeal for humility on the part of all. This leads to the kind of exaltation which brings sure relief from or in persecution. In the meantime, they should cast all their cares on God for He cares for them in their affliction (5:6-7). Behind all their suffering is the enemy, the devil, who, described under the metaphor of a roaring lion, seeks to destroy the believer and his testimony. Thus, there is a need for diligent watchfulness for this one who is constantly on the prowl. The wise method of winning over him is to "resist him, firm in your faith" knowing that believers everywhere are suffering similar affliction.

Peter brings his letter to a close with a benediction (5:10-11), information and greetings (5:12-13a), and a final wish: "Peace to all of you who are in Christ" (5:14b).

Use the exam sheet at the back of the book to complete your exam.

1. **Hebrews demonstrates the superiority of Christ over**
    A. the religion of the Greeks.
    B. the religion of the Romans.
    C. the religion of the Jewish people.
    D. the religion of the Arabs.

2. **The key word of Hebrews is**
    A. "better."   C. "blood."
    B. "righteousness."   D. "sacrifice."

3. **Hebrews is interspersed with several**
    A. encouragement passages.
    B. warning passages.
    C. correctional passages.
    D. prophetic passages.

4. **The one common denominator in all the "let us" passages is**
    A. living out the faith.
    B. God's chastisement of believers.
    C. the future hope of heaven.
    D. suffering for the sake of righteousness.

5. **The priestly ministry of Christ is superior to that of**
    A. Abraham.   C. Aaron.
    B. Moses.   D. Zadok.

6. **James is a very practical epistle which calls for a**
    A. hope that motivates endurance.
    B. faith that is genuine.
    C. love that is sincere.
    D. character that is holy.

7. **James used what two believers as illustrations showing the reality of faith by works?**
   A. Abraham and Rahab
   B. Joshua and Caleb
   C. David and Jonathan
   D. Boaz and Ruth

8. **The balance in handling the problem of materialism is to**
   A. give away everything we do not need.
   B. never seek a high paying job.
   C. consider God and His will in everything we do.
   D. tithe our material resources.

9. **Peter wrote his first epistle for the purpose of**
   A. condemning and warning rebellious believers.
   B. commending and praising faithful believers.
   C. reproving and rebuking carnal believers.
   D. comforting, encouraging, and instructing suffering believers.

10. **The general outline structure of 1 Peter shows that most of 1 Peter deals with**
    A. salvation, sanctification, and suffering.
    B. sin, shame, and suffering.
    C. sanctification, suffering, and glorification.
    D. salvation, eternal security, and suffering.

What Do You Say?

According to James what is the proof of genuine faith? What evidence do you have that you possess this faith?

----

2 Peter and 1, 2, 3 John

When comparing these four General Letters one finds a great deal of similarity in terms of emphasis. The church viewed from the perspective of Hebrews, James and 1 Peter was that of a persecuted and suffering church at the hands of its enemies on the outside. These last letters reveal that the church was threatened from within by false teachers from its own membership. Persecution from without and false teaching from within has always been a deep problem for the church of Jesus Christ throughout its 2,000-year history. Peter, John, and Jude give us help in knowing how to combat heresy and heretics.

THE SECOND LETTER OF PETER

The Author

Second Peter 1:1 states that this letter is from "Simeon Peter, a servant and apostle of Jesus Christ." There is no doubt that this is indeed the Apostle Peter for he speaks of himself as being on the Mount of Transfiguration with our Lord (1:16-18; Matt. 17:1-8).

The Readers

The readers are identified as to their spiritual condition rather than location. The question arises: "Are these the same readers to whom the first letter of Peter was sent?" The answer is yes. How do we know? Because in 3:1, Peter definitely states this to be the case: "This is now the second letter that I am writing to you, beloved …."

The Date and Occasion of Writing

Scholars date 2 Peter shortly after the writing of the first letter (around AD 66–67). The occasion was the assault of false teachers and their heresy. These false teachers are described, generally, as covetous (2:3) and those who walk after the flesh (2:10). The most serious aspect of their heresy is their denial of the deity of Christ (2:1), the blood atonement of Christ (2:1), and the second coming of Christ (3:4). Peter's antidote to false teaching is the gaining of true spiritual knowledge. In fact, the word "knowledge" and its forms (know, knowing, known, etc.) are used several times (1:2, 5-6, 8, 12, 14, 16, 20; 2:9, 20, 21; 3:3, 17-18). Knowing the content and meaning of God's Word is crucial to resisting false teaching and exposing it as not from God.

The Purpose of 2 Peter

Peter had three purposes in mind. His first purpose was to stir up his readers to grow in the qualities of Christian character (1:3-15). The second was to strongly warn the believers against heretics and their heresies (2:1-22). The third was to encourage them to be patient in their expectation of the Lord's return (3:1-14). These three purposes are still very relevant for modern believers.

The General Structure of 2 Peter

1. Challenge to Grow in the Qualities of Christian Character (1:1-21)
2. Condemnation of False Teachers and Their Heresies (2:1-22)
3. Coming of Jesus and its Sanctifying Effects (3:1-18)

The Flow of Development of 2 Peter

1. Challenge to Grow in the Qualities of Christian Character (1:1-21)

After Peter's salutation (1:1-2), he states that we have the basis for growth in the qualities of Christian character because God has given to us "His divine power" and "precious and very great promises" (1:3-4). Building upon this basis, the believer is to be diligent in cultivating faith, virtue, knowledge, self-control, perseverance, godliness, brotherly kindness, and love (1:5-7). This does not exhaust the list of Christian qualities, but they are evidently the ones Peter felt were needed in their situation. He announces that to have these qualities means a fruitful life, but not to have them signifies defective spiritual eyesight accompanied by a bad memory concerning the fact that they were purged from their old sins (1:8-9). It is good, then, to take inventory of their spiritual lives to see if they are growing in Christian virtue. If they are, they can be assured they will "never fail" in this life, and have confidence of an abundant entrance into the future kingdom of our Lord (1:10-11).

> **Practicing the truth, since it comes from God, is wisdom.**

Peter knows that his readers are not ignorant of the practical truths he has just communicated, but he also knows how forgetful the believer can be of them. So he has felt obligated to go over "old" truth for the purpose of inspiring fresh devotion. Even after he has gone to be with the Lord, he will still be reminding them through the printed page of his writings (1:12-15). The foundation of all that Peter ministered, spoken or written, was not "cleverly devised myths" but divine revelation. He received revelation by firsthand experience of being with Jesus and was an eyewitness of His transfiguration. But more than that, he had the prophetic word. This prophetic witness did not originate in man's will, but in the will of God, for "men spoke from God as they were carried along by the Holy Spirit" (1:16-21). Practicing the truth, then, since it comes from God, is wisdom.

2. Condemnation of False Teachers and Their Heresies (2:1-22)

Peter turns the spotlight on those who will communicate heretical teaching. These messengers of Satan secretively introduce destructive heresies which include denying the Lord and His atonement. With deception and greed they will take advantage of professing believers, leading them into error and immoral practices (2:1-3a).

These enemies of truth and righteousness will someday pay for their wickedness. Just as God, in His time, brought judgment against fallen angels (3b-4), against the pre-flood world (5) and against Sodom and Gomorrah (6–9), so He will punish the false teachers. In the process of judgment, He will save the righteous as He did Noah and Lot.

More definitively, these false teachers are arrogant, unreasonable, and immoral in their practices. Peter draws attention to their negative influence on others, their insatiable greed, and their religious deceptions. The sad thing is that some of them had some knowledge of Christ but had turned back to their old lifestyles. Peter says that it would have been better for them not to have known about Christ. They are pictured as a dog which returns to its own vomit!

3. Coming of Jesus and Its Sanctifying Effects (3:1-18)

The false teachers just mentioned in chapter two are not only proponents of heresies but also scoffers concerning the truth of God. Thus Peter calls for his readers to remember what the prophets and our Lord Jesus Christ had predicted concerning scoffers (3:1-2). The scoffers criticized the teaching of the Lord's coming. They cried out in their mockery, "Where is the promise of His coming?" They inferred by their sarcastic mocking question that the Lord was coldly indifferent to His promises. Peter says that they have put the wrong construction on the delay of the Lord's coming. They should interpret that delay as God's great mercy. In the meantime, God is exercising patience by giving people the opportunity to repent and escape the judgment (3:3-10).

> We should pursue peace and purity and account God's patient forbearance with this sinful world to mean the possibility of salvation for all.

In the light of coming judgment believers should be holy and godly. They should be expectant of the new creation wherein dwells righteousness. They should pursue peace and purity and account God's patient forbearance with this sinful world to mean the possibility of salvation for all. This was the way Paul viewed God's patience even though others had twisted the meaning of his letters. So be on guard and do not be led astray by false teachers. Rather, "grow in the grace and knowledge of our Lord and Savior Jesus Christ" (3:11-18).

THE FIRST LETTER OF JOHN

The Author

This letter of five chapters is anonymous (the author does not name himself). However, many of the church Fathers attributed it to the Apostle John. There are several literary similarities between this letter and the Gospel of John which give evidence that the author of the Gospel is also the author of 1 John. Two outstanding examples are the author's vocabulary and his literary style. That is, if one has read the Gospel of John a few times and then reads 1 John, he senses that he is reading material that comes from the same hand.

The Readers

The readers were not identified as to their geographical location or the church fellowship to which they belonged. One speculation of scholars is that John wrote this letter from the city of Ephesus, where he lived out the later years of his life, and that it was sent as a circular letter to the various churches of the Province of Asia. One thing is clear, and that is that John wrote to professing believers in Jesus.

The Date of Writing

Scholars generally agree that all of the Apostle John's writings were written sometime between AD 85 and 95.

The Purposes of 1 John

There seem to be several of these–some major and some minor. Let us note two major purposes.

The Assurance of Salvation

The key verse for this purpose is 1 John 5:13, which reads: "I write these things to you who believe in the name of the Son of God, that you may know that you have eternal life." It seems that the author of 1 John is intent on establishing the criteria whereby one can judge the reality of the salvation which he professes to have in Jesus Christ. In a human family,

166 NEW TESTAMENT SURVEY

children resemble their parents and one another. In God's spiritual family, true members will resemble their heavenly parent, God the Father. Among other things, God is characterized by holiness, righteousness, and love. If we truly belong to Him then we will be like Him in these family traits. You should ask yourself, "Do I bear these family characteristics?" If not, then why not?

A Warning Against False Teachers and Teaching

John, the Apostle, was quite concerned that the believers to whom he wrote would be unduly influenced by heresy. The heresy to which he referred had to do with the person of Jesus Christ and is reflected in 1 John 2:18-29 and 4:1-6. John wanted the believers to be able to distinguish between truth and error concerning the person of Christ, so that they would not be moved away from the very foundation of the Gospel. There were some who denied that Jesus was the Christ (2:22). These, John said, were liars and antichrists. Others were saying that Jesus Christ had not come in the flesh (4:3)—a reference to His historic incarnation. These false teachers, John says, are not of God.

> **God is light in 1 John in the sense that He is holy and pure.**

Some Themes of 1 John

John states his themes in contrast. For instance, Christ and the devil, light and darkness, love and hate, truth and lie, righteousness and lawlessness, life and death, and the Holy Spirit and demonic spirits. John states things in absolute terms. It is either one or the other. There is nothing in between. You either give your allegiance to Christ or you don't. You either follow the positive characteristics mentioned or you follow the negative. There is no middle ground as far as John is concerned.

The General Structure of 1 John

1. Introduction (1:1-4)
2. God Is Light (1:5–2:28)
3. God Is Righteous (2:29–4:6)
4. God Is Love (4:7–5:3)
5. Conclusion (5:4-21)

The Flow of Development of 1 John

1. Introduction (1:1-4)

John's introduction is intended to express the point that Jesus is absolutely a real person, not some phantom ghost as false teachers were preaching. John and the apostles actually saw Him, looked upon Him, and handled Him. They bore witness to Jesus who is the life, the Word of life, and the eternal life. They declared Him so that believers might have fellowship with them in the family of God and be filled with joy.

2. God Is Light (1:5–2:28)

God is light in 1 John in the sense that He is holy and pure. How may believers in Jesus Christ reflect this attribute of God in their lives? First, the believer must walk in the light—be pure (1:5-7). Secondly, the believers must recognize sin for what it is, deal with it when it arises in their own life, and know that in Christ sinners have an advocate with the Father (1:8–2:2). Thirdly, they must live obediently (2:3-11) keeping in mind their blessings of being forgiven, their experiential knowledge of the Father, and victory over the evil one (2:12-14). Fourthly, the believer is not to love the world (2:15-17) for to do so would show that the love of the Father is not in them. Fifthly, they are to be on the alert for false teachers who do not have the true teaching about the person of Jesus Christ. Walking in the light comprehends all these areas (2:18-28).

3. God Is Righteous (2:29–4:6)

Because God is righteous, believers are to practice righteousness in daily life. This section easily breaks down as follows: the root of practical righteousness is the new birth. In other words, living righteously is proof of our state of being born again into God's family (2:29). Secondly, there is the motive for practical righteousness, which is the wonderful fact of the Father's love for us—making us His dear children and giving us hope of being like His Son when He is revealed (3:1-4). Thirdly, we have the basis for practical righteousness, which is the work of Jesus Christ, the sinless one, removing our sin (3:5). Fourthly, and what is emphasized the most in this major section, we have the contrast of practical righteousness with the practice of sin and lawlessness (3:6-24). One should be careful to observe when reading this section that the emphasis in the contrast is on habitual practice, not isolated acts. One should observe as well, to avoid confusion, that the particular aspect of practical righteousness emphasized is love. Though love will be the major idea in the next major point, the apostle looks at it here as a by-product of practical righteousness. Fifthly, we have the responsibility of practical righteousness in the religious realm (4:1-6). Just because someone comes along and says that he is a Christian teacher with a message from God is not reason enough to listen to and believe that teacher and his message. What should be done? Because the world is filled with false prophets, the believer has the responsibility to put these people to the test. They are to test the spirits (prophets) to determine their origin—whether they are of God or not. The area of the test concerns the person of Christ.

4. God Is Love (4:7-5:3)

First, John says, because "God is love" we are to love one another (4:7-8). Everyone who loves, says John, proves he is born of God. Secondly, John mentions the greatest manifestation of love as seen in the historic death of Christ at the cross (4:9-10). As our propitiation, God removed His wrath from us and gave us life. Thirdly, we have the proper response to God's love—we ought to love one another (4:11). The privilege of love—intimate union with God—is next emphasized by John (4:12-16). It is the Holy Spirit who illuminates this (4:13). The aim of love is strong

The true mark of the professing believer in Jesus Christ is love.

confidence (4:17-18), for perfect love casts out fear. Finally, the highest evidence of love (4:19–5:3) is not mere words like "I love God" (4:20), but the keeping of God's commandments (5:2-3; compare John 14:21). The true mark of the professing believer in Jesus Christ is love. Jesus said, "By this all people will know that you are my disciples, if you have love for one another" (John 13:35). Let us then obey by loving as He loved us.

5. Conclusion (5:4-21)

John, in his conclusion, emphasizes strong faith (5:4-12). The one, John says, who overcomes the satanic world system is the one who "believes that Jesus is the Son of God" (vs. 4-5). To make sure his readers know whom he is speaking of, he further identifies the Son of God as the one who "came by water and blood"—water referring to Christ's baptism, and blood to the blood atonement (the beginning and ending of Christ's ministry, 5:6-12).

Secondly, John emphasizes strong confidence in the assurance of eternal life for those who believe (5:13), and confidence in prayer that is prayed in the will of God (5:14-17).

Thirdly, John gives assurance that the true believer is preserved from the wicked one (the devil) even though the whole world lies in his power (5:18-19).

Finally, John reminds his readers that the Son of God has truly come to this earth. The understanding that He has given us by virtue of His coming has made it possible for us not only to "know Him who is true," but also to be "in Him who is true, in His Son Jesus Christ. He is the true God and eternal life." With much good reason, then, John exhorts, "Little children, keep yourselves from idols" (5:20-21). There was much idolatry in the province of Asia where Ephesus was located. It was a great temptation for some believers. But there is much temptation to idolatry in our modern world. In reality, an idol is any vain, empty conception of God held by men. It includes all human substitutes for God. Actually, anything that takes the place which God should have in our lives is an idol. Do you have any idols in your life? Take John's advice: "keep yourselves from idols."

THE SECOND LETTER OF JOHN

The Author, Date and Readers

The author of this one chapter letter was the Apostle John. It was written sometime between AD 85–95. John addressed this very brief letter of 13 verses to the "elect lady and her children ..." (1:1). The "lady" is not identified by name and this has led to much speculation. Some think the term refers to the whole church. Certainly this little letter is good for the whole church! Others think the term means some local church which cannot now be identified today. Many take the term just to refer to some very important and influential Christian lady near to where the Apostle John lived and ministered. This makes good sense and seems to be the most obvious view. Not knowing exactly the recipients of the letter does not impair our understanding of it.

General Structure of 2 John

1. The Salutation—He Wishes Grace, Mercy and Peace (1:1-3)
2. Exhortation—To Walk in Love and Truth (1:4-11)
3. Conclusion—John Hopes to Visit the Elect Lady (1:12-13)

Purpose

The chief purpose is to warn believers against giving Christian hospitality to those who do not hold to the truth. If any of these should come to believers and not bring the true teaching concerning the person of Jesus Christ he is not to be received (1:7-11). Many cult groups send their missionaries door-to-door with their false message. These are to be refused entrance and hospitality. A secondary purpose (1:12-13) is to tell the "elect lady" of his plans to visit.

THE THIRD LETTER OF JOHN

Authorship, Date, and Readers

The Apostle John was the author of 3 John. He wrote it at the same time as 2 John—sometime between AD 85–95. He calls himself "the elder" and addresses it to "Gaius whom I love in truth" (1:1). There are several men by this name (Acts 19:29; 20:4; Rom. 16:23; 1 Cor. 1:14) making it impossible to identify this particular one. Whoever he was, John commends him for "walking in truth" (1:3), and for his good works to fellow believers (1:5-6).

General Structure of 3 John

1. Salutation (1:1-4)
2. Gaius Praised (1:5-8)
3. Diotrephes Condemned (1:9-10)
4. Demetrius Commended (1:11-12)
5. Conclusion (1:13-14)

Purpose of Writing 3 John

One purpose of John's letter was not only to encourage Gaius by praising him for his outstanding Christian testimony in walking in doctrinal truth and ministering to the needs of others, but also to encourage him to continue to do so. A second purpose was to reveal that he knows about the domineering influence of a professed believer by the name of Diotrephes who had brought evil into the church, and to say that he will deal with him if he comes for a visit. In the meantime he encourages the believers not to imitate Diotrephes' evil. A third purpose was to introduce Demetrius (who probably delivered this letter to Gaius), and to alert them to a coming visit from John.

One thing this short letter teaches us is to be humble servants like Gaius and not proud and arrogant like Diotrephes. Gaius patterned his life after the Lord, but Diotrephes after the devil.

LESSON 11 EXAM

Use the exam sheet at the back of the book to complete your exam.

1. **The occasion for Peter's second epistle was**
    A. the intense persecution experienced by the readers.
    B. the assault of false teachers on the readers.
    C. the planned visit of Peter to the readers.
    D. to give answers to perplexing problems.

2. **The false teachers denied the**
    A. Deity of Christ.
    B. blood atonement of Christ.
    C. Second Coming of Christ.
    D. all of the above.

3. **Peter's antidote to false teaching is**
    A. good works.   C. spiritual knowledge.
    B. confrontation.   D. trust through prayer.

4. **The foundation of all that Peter ministered was**
    A. human imagination.   C. legends.
    B. fables.   D. divine revelation.

5. **One purpose of 1 John was to**
    A. establish criteria to determine assurance of salvation.
    B. give the identity of the Anti-Christ.
    C. explain the nature of the Trinity.
    D. calculate the date for the second coming of Christ.

6. **The general outline structure of 1 John views the character of God as**
    A. light, righteousness, and love.
    B. sovereign and unchanging.
    C. merciful and kind.
    D. holy and wrathful.

7. **John's introduction (1 John 1:1-4) was intended to express the point that**
    A. the devil is always assaulting Christians.
    B. angels are servants of those who are saved.
    C. all people should be baptized.
    D. Jesus is absolutely a real person.

8. **John teaches that the root of practical righteousness is the believer's**
    A. study of Scripture.   C. new birth.
    B. good works.   D. all of the above.

9. **2 John tells us that whoever does not bring the truth concerning Christ's person**
    A. is not to be received.
    B. may be received with caution.
    C. is to be received with the hope that they will change.
    D. is to be received for the purpose of argument.

10. **3 John teaches us to be servants like**
    A. Demas.   C. Alexander.
    B. Diotrephes.   D. Gaius.

What Do You Say?

Why is the emphasis among the last four letters so important?

Jude and Revelation

THE LETTER OF JUDE

The Author

Who was Jude? Matthew 13:55 and Mark 6:3 relate that he was the brother of Jesus. Mark 6:3 says, "is not this the carpenter, the son of Mary and brother of James and Joses and Judas (Jude) ...." Jude does identify himself as a brother of James, but he does not call himself a brother of Jesus. Why? Because things have changed. Now, since the death, burial, resurrection, and ascension of Jesus things have changed. Now he calls himself simply "a servant of Jesus Christ."

The Date of Writing

2 Peter was written around AD 66–67 and Jude was written sometime after that. What is the reasoning for this assumption? It is based on content. In 2 Peter, the Apostle warned about the coming of false teachers (2 Peter 2:1). Jude definitely says that they have arrived: "For certain people have crept in unnoticed who long ago were designated for this condemnation, ungodly people, who pervert the grace of our God into sensuality and deny our only Master and Lord, Jesus Christ" (Jude 1:4). A specific date after AD 68 is uncertain. Scholarly opinion ranges anywhere from AD 68 to 85.

> **Jude, the brother of Jesus, calls himself simply "a servant of Jesus Christ."**

The Readers

The readers are not racially or geographically identified. Jude simply addresses them as "those who are called, beloved in God the Father and kept for Jesus Christ" (Jude 1:1). He wishes that "mercy, peace, and love be multiplied" to them (Jude 1:2).

The Purpose for Writing

Jude's original purpose was to write concerning the common salvation, but he changed his mind because of the pressing need to minister to them about contending earnestly "for the faith that was once for all delivered to the saints" (1:3). The expression "the faith" refers to the teaching of the Apostles ("apostles' teaching," Acts 2:42). Jude 1:4-16 makes it quite clear why there was a need for Jude to change his purpose. Much of this section is very much like 2 Peter 2.

The General Structure of Jude

1. Salutation (1:1-2)
2. Occasion for Writing—Need to Defend the Faith (1:3-4)
3. Sin and Doom of False Teachers (1:5-16)
4. Exhortation to the Faithful to Spiritual Growth and Soul-winning (1:17-23)
5. Doxology—Glory, Majesty, Wisdom, and Power Be to God Both Now and Forever (1:24-25)

Though Jude is a short letter, it packs a powerful message of judgment against apostates from the faith. The Lord is coming and He will judge (1:14-15)! Jude also challenges true believers to build up themselves in their faith, to pray in the Holy Spirit, and to keep themselves in the love of God while they are waiting for the mercy of our Lord to eternal life. A strong word of encouragement is given in the doxology, assuring the preservation of true believers in this life and assurance of standing blameless before Him in the next (1:20-24). May you be challenged and encouraged in your Christian walk by the message of Jude.

> Jude challenges true believers to build up themselves in their faith, to pray in the Holy Spirit, and to keep themselves in the love of God.

REVELATION

Imagine going to an art gallery where a new piece of art is going to be made public. When you arrive you see at the front of the auditorium an object which is totally veiled. You haven't the faintest idea what is under the covering, but you know the artist always creates something outstanding. So you wait with excitement for the appointed time when the veil will be removed and the masterpiece seen. The time arrives and the veil is removed. You are amazed at what you see and want to get closer so that you may study its outlines and details. Even with the closer look there is still much that is inscrutable and you know that it would take a long time to fathom the depths of its meaning.

The book of Revelation is parallel to this imagined story. The English word "revelation" comes from the Greek word *apocalypses,* meaning "to unveil" or "to uncover." Thus, the content of the book of Revelation is something which was hidden in the mind of God. Then at His appointed time it was unveiled or revealed to the Apostle John. What John discovered through the unveiling is now available to us 2,000 years later. It is God's great prophetic plan for the future.

The Author of Revelation

The author of Revelation identifies himself as John five times (1:1, 4, 9; 21:2, 8). Which John is this? The church fathers give very strong testimony that this John is the Apostle, son of Zebedee and brother of James.

John was on the Island of Patmos (see map on the next page) when he received the visions and revelations of this book. The church fathers tell us that he was exiled there because of persecution. In his own words, John says he was on Patmos "on account of the word of God and the testimony of Jesus" (1:9). Sometimes it is when we are in our deepest affliction that God blesses and uses us in great measure.

The Readers and Date of Writing

John wrote to "the seven churches" (see map). He was probably familiar with all these churches and had ministered to them, since he had lived in the city of Ephesus for many years. The churches were in Ephesus, Smyrna, Pergamum, Thyatira, Sardis, Philadelphia, and Laodicea. John wrote about AD 95 during the reign of Roman Emperor Domitian (AD 81–96). Domitian was a cruel persecutor of the church and the first one of the Caesars to officially declare himself God. This declaration was put on coins bearing his image.

The Occasion for Writing Revelation

This is very simple to determine. It was a direct command of the Lord (1:11, 19). Verse 11 says, "Write what you see in a book and send it to the seven churches."

The Theme and Purpose of Revelation

The grand theme of this book is Jesus Christ, and the purpose is to give to God's people a revelation of the person of Christ and His plan for the future. The author in the very act of revealing the future exalts the Lord Jesus Christ. Revelation not only reveals what our Lord Jesus Christ will do, but also what would be done for Him. The object of the book is to unveil the last stages of God's redemptive plan. These consist of the Second Coming of Jesus to earth, the establishment of the Kingdom of Christ for 1,000 years upon the earth, and the eternal state with its new heaven and

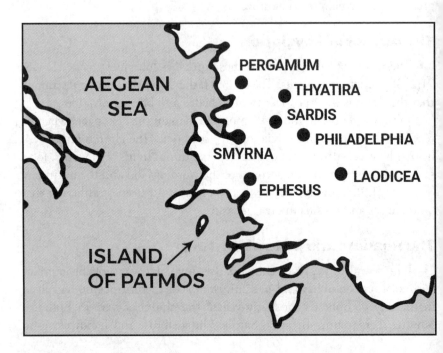

earth (see 11:15; 19:11–22:5). In all of this the Lord Jesus Christ is central, "for the testimony of Jesus is the spirit of prophecy" (19:10).

Some Points of Interest Regarding Revelation

- Revelation is the only book of the New Testament totally devoted to prophecy.
- Revelation is the only book of the New Testament to pronounce a special blessing on its readers, hearers, and doers (1:3).
- Revelation is the only book of the New Testament which pronounces a curse upon any who would add to or take away from this book (22:18-19).
- Revelation is the throne book of the New Testament. Out of the 60 times the word throne is found in the New Testament, 45 are in Revelation.
- Revelation puts a large emphasis on the number seven, such as seven churches, seven seals, seven trumpets, seven bowls, etc.
- Revelation quotes and alludes to the Old Testament more than any other New Testament book.
- Revelation and Daniel are closely related for they often deal with the same subject matter (compare Dan. 7 with Rev. 13).
- Revelation is highly symbolic. It contains symbols such as numbers, colors, precious stones, wild animals, stars, names, etc. These are used to represent various persons, events, things, truths, etc.

The Interpretation of the Book

Throughout the centuries of church history, Bible students have approached the interpretation of the book of Revelation differently. Some think, for instance, that it was entirely fulfilled in the early history of the church. Others believe that it is a book which has been in the process of being fulfilled throughout the whole Christian era. Still others hold that Revelation is not a record of actual events which have been fulfilled or which are going to come to pass; rather, it merely pictures the constant struggle throughout the church age between good and evil. A fourth interpretation, favored by this author, is sometimes labeled the futurist view. It holds that the greater part of Revelation (4–22) is yet to be fulfilled. The futurist view uses Revelation 1:19 as the inspired key in outlining the content of the book. Let us see this general structure in the next point based on that verse.

The General Structure of Revelation

1. The Past—"write therefore the things that you have seen" (1:1-20)
2. The Present—"those that are" (2:1–3:22)
3. The Future—"and those that are to take place after this" (4:1–22:21)

The Flow of Development of Revelation

1. The Past (1:1-20)

John saw an awesome vision of Christ as judge in Revelation 1. This vision portrays our Lord as walking in the midst of the churches scrutinizing their character and conduct. His evaluation is given in chapters 2 and 3.

2. The Present (2:1–3:22)

These chapters consist of seven letters from our Lord Jesus Christ sent to the seven churches of Asia (see map on previous pages). These are not symbolic, but seven actual churches existing in John's day. The letters had a direct bearing on their character and conduct, but one should not think that there is no interpretation and application for the churches today. In fact, the churches today need to study closely what our Lord said to these churches by way of commendation, condemnation, threat, and promise. It is a healthy thing for churches to pause and evaluate themselves in the light of Christ's person and standards. Modern churches which do so with an openness and willingness to change can expect God's blessing. Let us heed, then, the Savior's words, "He who has an ear, let him hear what the Spirit says to the churches" (2:7).

> It is a healthy thing for churches to pause and evaluate themselves in the light of Christ's person and standards.

3. The Future (4:1–22:21)

Introduction (4:1–5:14)

These chapters picture a marvelous scene in heaven. The church is there because it has been raptured to heaven. It is a scene of worship where the redeemed and myriad of angelic beings surround the throne of God and bring worship to Him who sits on the throne. This marvelous, peaceful, comforting scene, however, is the heavenly prelude to the pouring out of awesome judgments upon the earth. The scene switches from heaven to earth in chapter six and the judgments begin.

The Judgments of the Seven-Year Tribulation Period (6:1–9:10)

This is a time of the wrath of almighty God. Three series of judgments are predicted. These series are called the seal judgments, the trumpet judgments, and the bowl judgments. Each series consists of seven specific judgments. The earth has never seen anything like it. On occasions, the series are interrupted to give some specific prophecy concerning important future people or events. (Examples would be chapters 7, 10–14; 17–19.)

The Second Coming of Jesus (19:11-21)

Finally, Jesus will come. He will put down all rule and authority and rule with a rod of iron. The beast (the last anti-God world ruler) and the false prophet (his assistant) will be cast alive into the lake of fire (19:20). This coming of Jesus literally to earth is not to be confused with the rapture of the church to heaven taught by Paul in such passages as 1 Thessalonians 4:13-18.

The Kingdom and Final Judgment (20:1-15)

The earthly kingdom of our Lord will last for 1,000 years. Satan is bound during the kingdom period and then released upon its conclusion. He will attempt to deceive the nations once again, but will be unsuccessful for the Lord will cast him into the lake of fire where the beast and the false prophet already are. Then the last judgment, called "the great white throne" will be convened. Those whose names are not found in the book of life, showing they are not true believers, will be cast into the lake of fire. What a solemn scene. Let me ask you. Will you be in heaven someday with the Lord, or in the lake of fire with the devil? It is your choice. To choose Christ is to choose heaven. To refuse Him is to suffer forever in eternal torment.

The New Jerusalem (21:1–22:5)

Jesus said, "I go and prepare a place for you, I will come again and will take you to myself, that where I am you may be also" (John 14:2-3). Where is that place? It is the New Jerusalem. This section gives a glorious description of the city where we shall dwell with our Lord forever.

The Conclusion (22:6-21)

The book of Revelation closes first of all with comforting words (22:6-17). The most comforting is the assurance of Jesus that He is coming (6-7). Secondly, there are words of admonition which consist of a curse upon any who would add to or take away from the book (18-19). Lastly, John gives his benediction in which he mentions again the coming of Jesus. He then wishes for all the readers of Revelation that the grace of the Lord Jesus would be with all of them (20-21). This grace of our Lord is what saves us, sanctifies us, and empowers to live for Jesus while we wait His promised return.

LESSON 12 EXAM

Use the exam sheet at the back of the book to complete your exam.

1. **Jude's original purpose in writing his letter concerned**
   A. identification with Christ through baptism.
   B. their common salvation.
   C. spiritual unity by the Holy Spirit.
   D. being a faithful witness to Christ.

2. **The expression "the faith" refers to**
   A. personal faith.
   B. saving faith.
   C. the teaching of the apostles.
   D. Christianity as a religion.

3. **The English word *revelation* means to**
   A. discern.   C. scrutinize.
   B. unveil.   D. enlighten.

4. **The book of Revelation is God's great plan for the**
   A. past.   C. future.
   B. present.   D. our personal lives.

5. **Revelation is closely related to**
   A. Daniel.   C. Hosea.
   B. Jeremiah.   D. Malachi.

6. **The interpretation of Revelation favored by the author of this course is sometimes called the**
   A. historical view.
   B. allegorical view.
   C. futurist view.
   D. preterist view.

7. **The book of Revelation encompasses things which deal**
   A. with the past, present, and future.
   B. only with the present and the future.
   C. only with the past and the future.
   D. only with the future.

8. **The three series of judgment to be brought on the earth during the tribulation period (6:1–19:10) are called**
   A. chariots, lightening, and thunder.
   B. seals, trumpets, and bowls.
   C. white horses, red horses, and black horses.
   D. famine, destruction, and death.

9. **In Revelation 20, John wrote about the judgment of**
   A. Israel.   C. believers.
   B. the nations.   D. unbelievers.

10. **The New Jerusalem is**
    A. not a literal place.
    B. only symbolic of heaven.
    C. present-day Jerusalem.
    D. a prepared, literal place.

What Do You Say?

Why do you think the book of Revelation is worthy of diligent study?

_____

_____

_____

_____

He who testifies to these things says, "Yes, I am coming soon." Amen. Come, Lord Jesus. The grace of the Lord Jesus be with God's people. Amen.

—Revelation 22:20-21